DADDY COOL

PERKIS DAY 09187

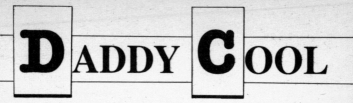

DADDY COOL

HOW TO RIDE A SEESAW WITH DIGNITY, WEAR A DONALD DUCK HAT WITH STYLE, AND SING "BINGO WAS HIS NAME-O" WITH PANACHE

Hugh O'Neill

Illustrations by Peters Day

WARNER BOOKS

A Warner Communications Company

The first page of "Beach Cool" appeared in Parents magazine, July 1985
Copyright © 1988 by Hugh O'Neill
All rights reserved.
Warner Books, Inc., 666 Fifth Avenue, New York, NY 10103

Printed in the United States of America
First Printing: June 1988
10 9 8 7 6 5 4 3 2 1

Library of Congress Cataloging in Publication Data

O'Neill, Hugh.
    Daddy cool: how to ride a seesaw with dignity, wear a Donald Duck
hat with style, and sing Bingo was his name-o with panache / Hugh
O'Neill.
        p.   cm.
    ISBN 0-446-38584-0 (pbk.) (USA.) / 0-446-38585-9 (pbk.) (Canada)
    1. Fathers—Anecdotes, facetiae, satire, etc.   I. Title.
PN6231.F37054 1988
818'.5402—dc19   87-30380
                                                              CIP

Illustrations by Peters Day
Design by Richard Oriolo

TO THE ORIGINAL

CONTENTS

PETERS DPY 99 87

INTRODUCTION

OUR HEROES HAVE NEVER BEEN DADDIES

Our heroes have never been daddies. Consider the pantheon of manliness—the granite-jawed Randolph Scott, Eastwood, the Duke, Alan Ladd as Shane, the outlaws Bogart and Cagney, the denim cool James Dean, not to mention Springsteen. All the legends have one thing in common. They are entirely undomesticated. Did Cagney ever buckle in a car seat? Did Cary Grant ever have oatmeal on his shoes? No. Cool is Muhammad Ali in his prime; Daddy is Ozzie Nelson. Cool is the open road to wherever it leads; Daddy is the station wagon to the swap meet.

The fact is that any fool can be cool when he's well rested, well-groomed, when he makes the decisions about his life. But it takes real sand to be cool when you haven't slept since June, when the Burl Ives version of "Little White Duck" is threatening to drive you mad, when you've just been awakened with a GoBot to the head. *Daddy Cool* is for any man who ever said "horsey" to a grown-up; any man who ever insisted that the new Care Bears movie is a homage to Godard; any man who ever

reached into his pocket for a business card and handed the best prospect he's had all year Mr. Potatohead's eyeglasses; any father who has been cut off from his mythology; any father who aspires to the flair of Astaire, the swagger of Jagger.

Over the last decade we have sold ourselves down the river of "fathering." We have wrapped ourselves in Snugglies, worn party hats, crawled, cuddled and bonded, kept diaries and actually said out loud that we're less interested in building empires than we are in being *there* for the kids. We have traded in our traditional right to be remote and mysterious—otherwise known as cool—for the right to wear a Donald Duck hat on command. Bad deal. It's time for a counterrevolution; it's time to put some style back in the big guy.

Make no mistake, *Daddy Cool* isn't modern. It isn't any of that I'm-strong-because-I-can-admit-I'm-weak stuff. *Daddy Cool* is a guide to good, old-fashioned, I'm-in-charge-here, drink-it-neat, deal-the-cards, here's-looking-at-you-kid cool. But it's a domesticated version, a code of cool for the guy with teethmarks on his wallet, offered in the hope that we might salvage something of our cowboy past and that our women might not forget the mugs for whom they took the fall.

Daddy Cool is a father's guide to combining the old cool moves with the flat-out uncool fact of the next generation, a handbook of hope, dedicated to the contrary proposition that not only is fatherhood not fatal to cool but that done right it's the greatest showcase for grace under pressure since Moses took all his children into the desert.

PLAYGROUND **C**OOL

How to Ride a Seesaw With Both Your Dignity and Your Child Intact

Children just flat love playgrounds—the swinging, sliding, spinning invitation of monkey bars and crawling tubes. Consequently, no decent father can avoid them. And yet, customized as they are for creatures of tiny limb, playgrounds are tough turf. They physically denature grown-ups, especially large male ones.

The Art of the Seesaw

Seesaws—designed to be shared by two people of approximately the same weight—are great tests of paternal ingenuity. Your four-year-old daughter weighs thirty-seven pounds—somewhere between 1/4 and 1/7 of your weight. So you've got to figure out a way to put between thirty-five and forty-two pounds of your body on your end of the seesaw. Any less and she drops suddenly to the ground, biting her tongue and vowing to tell Mommy what you did. Any more and you'll be telling the police that the last

time you saw her she was directly overhead and headed for the expressway. Now, if they'd let you put just part of your body on the seesaw you might be fine—throw one leg over your end of the plank, perch on it with one cheek. But kids won't let you get away with that. "That's not the right way, Daddy. No, Daddy, like this," they'll say, as though they think you don't know how to ride a seesaw. So what happens? You end up crouching awkwardly down over a two-by-eight that slaps you over and over again in the crotch as you desperately try to move her smoothly up and down. To top it off, you actually hear yourself saying, "Whee."

Some advice:

1. Don't hate yourself. This happened to you because you love your daughter more than you do your self-respect.

2. If Mommy is with you, suggest that she share the baby's

end of the seesaw. Right after he got out of the bathtub, Archimedes did some work with seesaws and came up with what is to this day known as the First and Only Law of Seesaws:

Mother + 4-year-old = close enough to Daddy.

Of course, this equalization of weight doesn't solve your problem. You are still, after all, sitting on a seesaw saying "Whee." But it does eliminate the stupid-lookingness that a great disparity of weights always creates.

3. Ask your wife if she would please chirp "Whee." She won't mind; if she loves you she'll know what you're going through and squeal loud enough to satisfy not only Bettina but every kid in the playground. If she asks why or flat refuses, get carefully off the seesaw, head out of the playground to the bus station, and when you get to Scranton, immediately begin (a) custody proceedings and (b) the search for a woman who knows the slightest thing about the difficulty of being a male enslaved by moronic concerns about image.

4. Just relax. Stop assuming everybody's looking at you and thinking what a drip you are. Content yourself with wondering whether she'll someday design a home heating system that employs a principle she first learned on a seesaw at the expense of your overrated dignity.

SURVIVING THE SLIDE

If you feel you must ride a sliding board, always be alert for the perilous Daddy Friction at the bottom. You see, a six-year-old is light enough so that his downward thrust overcomes the flat part at the bottom and allows him to dismount from the slide with a long-jumper's flourish. Fathers, however, weigh just enough so that they slide slowly, pathetically, anticlimactically to a stop. It's God's form of slow motion, stop action, his way of being sure that everybody has a chance to look at you, to see a man in wing tips hunching forward as kids bang into him from the back and whine, "Move, mister."

Your best defense against the Fatal Friction is to reach forward in the middle of the slide, grab the sides and pull yourself savagely forward in the manner of the Olympic bobsled team launching itself down the Maria Theresa run at Innsbruck. Of course, the risk is that you'll propel yourself right through the landing area and bounce off the metal mushroom. But that's small stuff considered beside the languorous agony of just plain sitting there as mothers gesture toward you, wondering if you're somebody's father or just a guy in a suit who likes to hang around the park.

My own most fearful experience in a playground took place inside a big bronze Mad Hatter–style top hat. Josh was a mere pup, fifteen months old or so, when he peeked into the top hat and, apparently liking what he saw, ventured in. Planning to reach in and retrieve him, I bent over the little Lewis Carroll door and peered in. In three seconds Josh had vanished inside the hat. Overcome by the certainty that some prestidigitator—realizing my son was the last best hope of humankind—had snatched him through some secret passage, I squeezed myself through the midget hole and into the hat. The instant I was in there, squatting like a duck, I came face-to-face with Josh, who had hidden himself in a little Lewis Carroll cove. With our faces no more than six inches apart, he began to laugh in that pure baby way, as though he thought the two of us in the hat was about the finest thing that a boy could wish for.

I panicked. I had a flash that this was where I would die, facing my laughing son while thrashing my seventy inches to exhaustion and death in a bronze top hat. I began to hyperventilate and tried to waddle out of the door, which had shrunk behind me. I banged my head, sending a clang ringing through the millinery tomb from which I would need to be cut by a torch, and sending Josh, who thought Daddy was so funny, into a laugh seizure that began as life itself and bounced bronzely back and forth until it became the sound track from a Stephen King film.

Dear reader, I survived and here offer the lesson of the Ringing Crypt, the most important rule about small places and fully grown men.

The Daddy Duck-Walk Avoidance Rule

Unless you're escaping from a life-threatening situation, never go anywhere that requires waddling like a duck. Your children will invite you to do so, beckoning you to join them inside the dinosaur. Don't be seduced by their apparent enthusiasm for you. That place which for them is a land of dreams is for you a muscle cramp .waiting to happen.

SONG **C**OOL

OF TONY BENNETT AND THE SCAT DADDY

Among the unchronicled changes that come with fatherhood is its impact on what you sing in the shower. Before fatherhood most of us cut loose while naked with some manly stud-duck numbers—a Sinatra croon about loving and losing, a blue-collar Springsteen belter about molten iron. But once we're Daddy, our repertoire of cool songs gets polluted by kid stuff. Suddenly the tough-guy ballad, the martial strain in our hearts, is competing for airtime with kid songs—a clucking, mooing, spelling, honking, counting album of monotonal cheerfulness that without your permission bores into your long-term memory. Old Blue Eyes's version of "New York, New York" segues into "The Itsy-Bitsy Spider." When cruising at flank speed on I-95 "Jumpin' Jack Flash" turns into "This Old Man," a preposterous psychotropic ditty about a fella who apparently played something called knick-knack on somebody's hive.

This is no mere inconvenience; it's a medical nightmare. We're attuned to the sound of the mournful sax. Who can

doubt that giving ourselves over to the Fisher-Price xylophone is the path to madness?

My own odyssey out of this musical quagmire is instructive. As always, Mr. Rogers was the occasion of hope.

Like most fathers, I've spent my fair share of time in the neighborhood of PBS's Fred Rogers, the affable cardigan-clad fellow who makes it perfectly clear to children that they can't go down the bathtub drain. And so I had been exposed to his trademark sign-off song, "It's You I Like," which can be most charitably described as a sappy little atonal nonrhyming ditty which, God bless it, gives kids permission to be nerds. One day while getting dressed for work I overheard what was unmistakably the voice of Tony Bennett singing something which had the same lyrics as Mr. Rogers' drip anthem. As I turned to look at the TV, Josh, apparently confused that some strange man was singing Mr. Rogers' song in a silly way, was preparing to change the channel in search of a Baby Muppet. "Just a second, son," I said, staying his hand and listening in astonishment as T.B. turned "It's You I Like" into the most potent scat love song I'd ever heard. Of course, I thought, as always both humbled by and proud of an insight, it's all in how you sing it. It's a matter—as cool guys throughout the ages have known—of style.

So herewith a guide to song cool, to saving ourselves from "Zippety Doo-Dah," to customizing those insistent kiddie songs for the stylish riffs in our hearts. With a tip of the paternal hat to Tony Bennett, a lesson about making music of the mundane.

SONG COOL

How to Turn a Kid's Ditty into "The Lady Is a Tramp"

I. Whenever a Song Has an Animal Sound, Substitute a Jazz Scat Riff.
Instead of the onomatopoeic clucking and barking, give 'em a quick taste of the Velvet Fog, Torme at his best. So "Old MacDonald" is changed from "with a moo-moo here/and a moo-moo there" to "with a bopaty-doo-wop here/and a shooby-doo-wop there."

II. Add Notes for Emphasis Where They're Least Expected.
"Bingo Was His Name-o" should be changed from "B-I-N-G-O" to "B, I say, I, I say N-G-O, and Bingo, yes, that was his name-o." Sinatra is the master of the ragged, rushed and yet somehow smooth extra lyric.

III. Whenever Possible, Use 1950s Hipsters Slang.
Instead of "This old man, he played nine," try "This old man, this cat played nine." Instead of "Kumbaya, my Lord, kumbaya," try "Kumbaya, my man, kumbaya."

The Torme, Sinatra, Bennett Daddy Cool Rendition of "Row, Row, Row Your Boat"

Row, I say, row, row that boat so-o-o-o
Gently down that stream
Merrily, merrily—shooby-doo-wop
Life [four-second pause] ain't nothin', no
Life [three-second pause]
Life, that lady's a dream.

With Apologies to Run/DMC: The Lullabye Rap Version

"I say row that boat
Now don't be slow.
You need a way to get there,
Here's the way to go.
I say row that boat on down the stream,
Let's row it together, we're a part of the team.
Merr-i-ly that's the way it should be,
And here's the situation that I want you to see:
Life's no scam, life's no scheme,
Please go to bed and have sweet dreams."

Every chance you get, listen to one of the great manly ones—be it Bennett or Woody Guthrie. When everybody else is asleep, sit in the dark in your underwear, tending a glass of plain old whiskey, and attend to some of the sounds. Drive away the frolic and chirp, tune yourself to the banter and the wail.

Private Music

In the spirit of making legends, be sure to have family songs. In our family "Red, Red Robin" reminds Rebecca that life has meaning. That song and that song alone—sung by Mommy or Daddy or Josh—makes the baby blues disappear without fail.

Just sing.

C AR C OOL

*HOW TO DRIVE
LIKE THE MAN YOU WERE*

We all know the pre-child Jack Kerouac driving fantasy. On the road, born to be wild, looking for adventure, wind through the hair, horizon in the eyes. But once you're a father, driving is never the same. Suddenly what were your wheels become nothing more than a car. Suddenly cruising with tunes—hitting the highway with the Silver Bullet Band—gives way to "Polly Wolly Doodle" as you shuffle off to Buffalo. Suddenly you're no longer downshifting through that turn but using your brakes, creeping dutifully homeward with the next generation. Suddenly life in the fast lane is something that happens on your left.

Fact: *When your car is moving you can't be what you once were.*

Hope: *Your car isn't always moving. And when it's standing still, you can trot out the old cool you.*

1. In a Traffic Jam

You're stuck in traffic, dead-stop, gridlock, the kids are

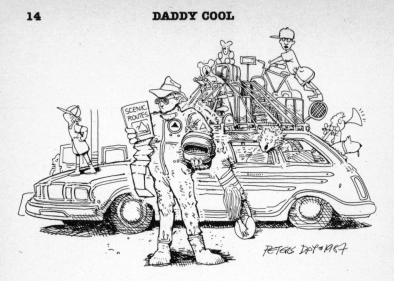

PETERS DPP 1987

wailing that they're going to die in the Lincoln Tunnel from a little carbon monoxide. Get calmly out of the car, pop the hood, wipe your hands across the back of your neck à la Henry Fonda in *The Grapes of Wrath*, fiddle with the spark plugs, which require absolutely no attention, and shamble back toward your seat, all the while looking forward and backward over the line of cars, in the manner of Ward Bond eyeballing the wagon train.

Why, you say? Well, you see, you're not supposed to get out of your car, not to mention tune it up, in the middle of traffic. Doing just that sends a powerful message that you write the music here, thank you very much. Your kids will treat it like an adventure and stop yelling long enough to ask you how you fixed the car. Your wife will feel better about you in general.

2. At Gas Stations

Get out of the car and talk to the kid who's pumping gas as though you're nostalgic for the days when you had his job, when life was as decent as an oil change and lube job. Presume that you guys are brothers-in-spirit, loving cars the way you do. Refer to your car as "she." Remember, however, that though calling your car "she" is cool, calling your car a proper name, say, "Beth," is not.

A DIGRESSION ON GASOLINE

Never buy anything less than a full tank of gas. While the expression "Fill 'er up" makes children for a moment forget about nuclear winter, the phrase "May I have six dollars' worth of unleaded" makes them concur with Hobbes that life is solitary, poor, nasty, brutish and short. Give them hope. Remember: *These are your children*.

You say you've only got ten dollars? In that case hand the kid the bill with a flourish and say, "Burn it all, pally."

Indeed, a case can be made that a truly cool father never takes his wife and kids to a gas station at all but gases up and checks the oil before setting out in the morning while they're eating their Egg McMuffins. It may be worth creating the impression that the car runs, not on fossil fuel, but because Daddy's behind the wheel.

BREAKDOWN COOL

When driving never use the sentence "Do you hear a funny clicking noise, doll?" Good God, fella, you hear the noise. You know it's real. Why point it out to your wife? You might as well tell her that she could die a protracted bed-ridden death without a friend. Think about it. It's midnight, eight degrees outside, you're thirty-seven miles from the nearest exit. What possible good can come of pointing out to your wife that your car, which is carrying your children, may collapse long before you get to Butte? Just drive. Sing. Drown out the noise. Keep it to yourself. That's strictly need-to-know stuff.

WHY DADDY IS THE WHEEL

There are three circumstances under which you let your wife drive and you become a passenger:

a. You've had a drink.
b. You're tired.
c. You've failed the road test three times.

I know this is an old-fashioned attitude. On a ten-hour trip to the Land of a Thousand Animals there is no reason in the world why you shouldn't split the driving with Edna. Or is there? Consider the contrast between the moment you arrive home as the driver and the moment you arrive home as a passenger.

> SCENE: It's midnight. You've been in and out of the car since noon, seeing America from Gary, Indiana, to Philly. Biff and Philomena are cuddled up, little-kid tired, subdued by brand-new memories of the Sandburgian heartland. Tomorrow's clouds are gathering. Your family is a drowsy timeless possibility on wheels, a brave certain little secret, thumping through the I-80 night.

Here's what happens if you drive:

You arc into the driveway. Your wife stirs beside you, sitting up suddenly, getting her bearings. "We're home, Monica," you say, reaching over, touching the impression the upholstery has made on her cheek. You surge out of the car, catching the scent of however-humble all-yours home, and say, "I'll get the kids, sweet. You go up." You reach in and unbuckle him. He smells sticky and sour. You imagine him someday carrying his own son. And then, into his bed, sandals flipped off. Then back to her. A screech in sudden protest, a mew, an arm flopping for no good reason at her side and into the crib, the one it took you too long to assemble. And then, a glimpse in passing at M., your partner in time, cuddled on top of the covers, Pittsburgh T-shirt and no pants, those legs doing to you what they've always done to you. And for you before sleep, a taste of whiskey and a lonesome early-morning toast to being home and the guy who—aware that the universal thump is forever afoot—got us there.

Here's what happens if your wife drives:

You sense a stop. You bolt awake. You shout, "That pitch was high, ump," realize where you are and say, "Oh, I see, this is our house, yeah, our house, right?" You take something from your wife. You think it's a child. You stagger upstairs and fall asleep with your shoes on.

Take your choice. Bottom line: *There is nothing cool about being a passenger.* Bogey never was, unless he was holding a gun on the driver.

CHAOS ON THE LONG ISLAND EXPRESSWAY

It will happen. The only question is when. Some parents believe the explosion is preceded, like an earthquake, by a period of preternatural calm, an ironic overture to nightmare. It usually begins like this:

"Jonah, don't throw things in the car. It's dangerous."

"Okay, Mommy, but my tummy hurts."

And within seconds four things happen:

1. What had moments ago been an empty highway turns into a traffic-choked nightmare.

2. The air temperature goes up fourteen degrees or to 99.7, whichever is higher.

3. What had been two crumb-covered angels turn into Martha and George from *Who's Afraid of Virginia Woolf?*

4. Your wife goes into shock, starts muttering something about having been so happy as a child.

What do you do?

1. Rush your wife to the hospital and describe to the admitting nurse how on your wedding day your wife's very laughter was like champagne.

2. Scream at the top of your voice that you'll kill everybody in the car unless (a) they stop making noise or (b) she starts behaving like the girl you married.

3. Louder than you've ever sung anything in your life, in the manner of Attila the Hun in the shower, start to sing "The Battle Hymn of the Republic," or any other song with the phrase "trampling out the vintage."

Answer Analysis

Answer 1 is wrong. You need not worry about your wife's health. Her affliction is temporary, a defense mechanism against the madness.

Answer 2 is also wrong. Cool guys don't yell. They also don't *threaten* to kill people. Talk is cheap.

Answer 3 is the Daddy Cool answer. Remember, these are not reasonable people. Fact: You can no more stop the juvenile chaos that has erupted in your car than you can hold back the tide. The trick is not to fight it, but for a moment go with it. Give up everything you've ever learned about civilized behavior. Go wild with your children, play on their terms.

The key is volume. You've got to show them that going berserk doesn't frighten you at all. They need to know they can't intimidate you with a little primordial madness. You've been to 'Nam, man. Who do these kids think they're dealing with? To see Daddy, the very symbol of order, behaving like the bass player from Twisted Sister is powerful stuff. It gets their attention. Once you stun them out of the screaming mode, your wife will come out of her coma and the two of you will have a shot at organizing a sing-along till home.

HOW TO SURVIVE
A FRED FLINTSTONE
INNER TUBE

It happened several years ago but the memory remains an open wound.

I like to think it was the Goofy hat that proved my undoing. I like to believe that but for the hat with the floppy black dog ears, I might have appeared to her like any other man staggering across the beach. But I know that isn't true. I know it was more than the hat.

Her eyes, those great womanly chocolate-brown lamps, told the whole ugly story about what fatherhood had done to me. There was no second look. She couldn't face the sight of another human turned into a donkey. She couldn't face the playpen I carried under one arm. She couldn't face the basket of pails and shovels. She couldn't face the kite, the beach umbrella, the thermos full of white grape juice. She couldn't face the Fred Flintstone bottle sticking out of my pocket. And she couldn't face that hat—that yellow and black monstrosity of cute.

I'll never forget her expression, the elemental sadness of those eyes. Suddenly bone-weary, I stumbled on, a vision of manliness denatured by Daddy stuff, a clattering heap of plastic in search of a place to sit down.

It was the lowest point of fatherhood. After that incident I was depressed for a week. I was, it seemed to me, nothing I had prepared to be. I was Dagwood Bumstead and Ozzie Nelson rolled into one. Still, after a few weeks my heart began to heal, sensing somehow that I had taken life's best shot. Looking back, I understand my mistake. I had assumed the beach was like any other place. Wrong. Fact: *It is impossible to be cool around people who are nearly naked.* Think about it.

Which of the following movie stars made their reputation in beach movies?

1. John Wayne
2. Jimmy Cagney
3. Sylvester Stallone
4. Clint Eastwood
5. Annette Funicello

The only beach John Wayne was ever on was Omaha. Try to imagine Jimmy Cagney putting on SunBlock. No, the beach is for women and kids. In fact, there are only three times in a man's life when being on the beach is cool:

1. It's midnight, you're seventeen, and she seems willing to believe you're not like all the rest of those jerks.

2. It's 6:30 A.M. and you and your campaign manager are walking on the beach (in wing tips) awaiting the returns from the coast.

3. You are the first person of your general racial type to ever walk on this beach.

Still, the wife and kids are the point, so . . .

THE THREE COMMANDMENTS OF BEACH COOL

I. Thou Shalt Not Imitate a Sea Creature.
Trust me on this one. They won't respect you for your octopus.

II. Thou Shalt Not Try to Get Sand off a Sandwich.
It never works. Just tell the kids that's why it's called a sandwich.

III. Thou Shalt Never Chase a Runaway Beach Umbrella.
I know, an umbrella tumbling across a jam-packed

beach looks dangerous, but in fact it's much less dangerous than a man leaping through Scrabble players screaming, "Excuse me, but my umbrella's on the fly."

BEACH COOL
MULTIPLE-CHOICE TEST

Question 1: The kite breaks, suddenly swooning to earth with a thwoosh. You:

1. Ask the kids what they think you should do now.
2. Tell the kids kites are stupid anyway.
3. Tell the kids you'll buy them a new one tomorrow.
4. Tell the kids that now Kitey will make a perfect mask—just like the ones the people in New Guinea wear.

Answer Analysis

Answer 1: Lots of guys choose this option—under the influence of that kids-are-just-little-adults idiocy. Bad idea. If you ask the kids what they think you should do, they'll suggest being cranky and whining about how now that Kitey is broken, life tastes like ashes.

Answer 2: This option has a certain Bogart appeal. But it's too tough. Remember an important Daddy Cool Mantra: *These are your children.*

Answer 3: Nope. Ecologically unsound.

Answer 4: This is the Daddy Cool answer. It's inventive, improvisatory, turns a crisis into a lesson in comparative culture and exotic geography.

Question 2: Your son asks you why the sand castle you made doesn't have detail—the stupid little designs, the working drawbridge, the catapult—like the one made by the daddy over there. You:

1. Tell him your gifts are not in the plastic arts.

2. Tell him it's better to use his imagination—to imagine that yours was a decent castle.

3. Tell him you don't think the castle over there is any great shakes.

4. Say, "Fine, maybe you'd like to be that guy's little boy."

Answer Analysis

None of these answers has anything to recommend it. You're on your own, boyo.

OLD PLAID BAGGY BATHING SUIT
vs.
ONE OF THOSE EUROPEAN BIKINI THINGS

Daddy Cool Beach Commandment:

Thou Shalt Not Wear a Bathing Suit Which Reveals Anything at All About the Part of Your Body It's Supposed to Conceal.

Believe it or not, lots of fathers actually appear on the beach, and in front of their children, wearing those little bikini bathing suits. You know, those flimsy numbers that brag about the pelvic region and thighs. They are completely unacceptable, not the slightest bit cool. Why, you ask? You're in good shape, run twenty-five miles a week, tummy's flat, cheeks still have some boyish curve. It doesn't matter. What kind of shape you're in has nothing to do with it. Under all circumstances this kind of hip-hugging exposure is a no-win situation. Consider four scenarios: The impact of a bikini bathing suit worn by a father with each kind of body on children of each gender.

Inner Thoughts of a Male Child When Seeing His Steel-Stomached Praxitelean Triathlon-Trained Father in a Bikini: "That's what God meant a man to look like. I'll never be the man my father is."

Response of Same Male Child When Seeing a Pastry-Shaped Rubenesque Father in the Same Suit: "Oh my God, Dad."

Inner Thoughts of a Female Child on Seeing Steel-Stomached Praxitelean Triathlon-Trained Father in a Bikini: "Oh my God, Daddy looks gorgeous. I'll never grow up from my current nine-year-oldness and find such a man with whom I can make children and build a life."

Inner Thoughts of Same Female Child on Seeing Pastry-Shaped Rubenesque Father in the Same Suit: "Oh my God, Daddy."

Simply put, there is just no paternal upside to this kind of bathing suit. If you look great, your overwhelming maleness will suffocate either a son or a daughter. If you look like hell, it's an assault on the sensibilities of everybody on the beach.

If you insist on tipping your hat to fashion, you can get a designer boxer-trunk swimsuit—one of those that feature muted earth tones with just enough pink and yellow splashed around to show you're not a complete drone. But why compromise? Don't choose a middle ground. Get yourself one of those big old green-and-black-plaid, thigh-and-crotch-concealing Eisenhower-era shrouds that you can wear up around your belly button with pride. It's a defiant gesture that sends the most powerful cool ''Who cares?'' message of all.

OF EINSTEIN,
DARWIN AND THE
BICAMERAL CHILD

Children are famous for asking tough questions about the natural world. Because their minds are undiminished by years of assumptions about momentum and moonlight, they'll often say things like "I know what a clock is, Daddy, but what is time?" Josh recently asked me a question about why his body was not attached to mine and ascended, question by question, to one that amounted to a query about nature's ability to differentiate anything from anything else. Further, science seems to mean Daddy. Mommy may be an internist at Mt. Sinai and Daddy a mime, but the natural world remains an atavistic Daddy obligation.

There is, of course, no way you can actually answer all their questions. After all, even Nobel Prize–winning daddies don't know what the Big Bang banged with. Kids have an uncanny instinct for the fundamental. Ultimately they'll chase you back into a corner and you'll have to confess that despite our technological achievements—despite

satellites and Velcro—we dwell in darkness. It's easy to look bad. That's not cool.

The temptation is to duck the question or, worse, make up answers. I once heard a father tell his daughter that waves were made by a sea monster rolling over in his sleep. She, God bless her, was having none of it and averred that that couldn't be right because the waves would be, in that case, rather more intermittent. Kids won't put up with fey answers. Believe me, the same boy who insists that the oak tree out back is a magic wand will, two hours later, in response to the answer "As much as a million and one elephants" say that he would prefer an answer in metric tons.

Simply put, to questions that indicate curiosity about the natural world, or what is commonly known as reality, *you may not give a goofy answer.* To the question "May I have a mushy egg sandwich, Daddy?" it's perfectly all right to answer, "The Amazing Mumford made all the eggs disappear," but in response to questions about the gestation period of a fox, that kind of frivolity is wimp stuff.

SCIENCE COOL QUIZ

QUESTION: "Daddy, what makes a rainbow?"

ANSWER: 1. "The angels are having a painting party in the sky."

2. "On Wednesdays the earth spins from left to right, thereby creating a color vacuum in the African hemisphere."

3. "How the hell should I know? What do I look like, Mr. Wizard?"

4. "Because the white light from the sun shines through the raindrops, which act as lenses refracting the light into its constituent colors, ranging from infrared to ultraviolet."

QUESTION: "Daddy, why does a zebra have stripes?"

ANSWER: 1. "Because God thought stripes were pretty."

2. "Because zebras are descended from a line of penguins."

3. "Ask your mother."

4. "Stripes are a kind of camouflage and make it more difficult for predators—especially lions—to spot the zebras among the tall variegated grasses of the African

plains. Consequently those African ungu-
lates that had such stripes were not eaten
by lions and survived to pass on their
genes.''

Of course, to both questions, number 4 is the only cool
answer. True, your son will be baffled by words like
"refract," and by the idea that light is composed of many
colors. Indeed, you may even stun yourself with the word
"ungulate." But no matter. The boy will realize that his
emerging brain has some work to do if it's to understand
anything. And more important, he'll know that Daddy can
be relied upon to give it to him straight, which is, after all,
what cool is all about.

PATERNAL ZOOLOGY: OF MICE AND MEN

Children have a special relationship with animals. It's no
coincidence that when kids are born, all of Mom and
Dad's friends swamp them with stuffed animals, totems of
the creature kingdom. Their enthusiasm for animals begins
with ducks and mice and ascends eventually in a Jungian
arc through dinosaurs to grizzly and polar bears in the
nine-year-old male.

Any father who hopes to be at all cool will have to
appear to be an animal expert. During the early years, the
charade is that you're a personal friend of Old MacDonald.
Later it's that you're a timber wolf post-doc from Montana
State, Bozeman campus.

The general idea is to use sleight of hand, to make
yourself appear to know more animal junk than you do.
You can rely on one of two techniques:

1. The Single-Species Strategy

A story is told about a father who made a point of learning
everything he could about wolves. He read dozens of
books, watched documentaries on PBS and would pass
along tidbits over the dinner table, saying things like,
"Jennie, did you know that the male gray wolf, who used
to roam free throughout the North American continent, is
now reduced to wandering a latitudinous band between
North Dakota and Alberta?" About other species he knew
less than nothing, but about wolves he made Kipling's
Mowgli look like a city kid.

The point is that the single-species strategy allows the
kids to assume that wolves are not Dad's only animal but
merely his favorite.

2. The Single-Trait Strategy

Some fathers are knowledgeable about a particular *trait*
of many different species. My father, for example, was
preoccupied with speed. I remember him telling me the
cheetah was the fastest land animal in the world. The next
day he clarified and told me I should understand that a
cheetah was the fastest for a short burst but that the
thoroughbred horse could outrun a cheetah over half a
mile. My father could handicap a 10K between a hippo
and a yak.

The point is, if your kids remember you as knowledgeable about animals, they'll subconsciously make the leap
to thinking you're a brilliant hunter-tracker and therefore a
provider. That's elemental. They'll associate you with
bringing home the bacon, which is the ultimate cool.

Some Are More Cool Than Others

With the exception of domesticated fowl, all animals are cool in their way. But, as George Orwell said, some are more equal than others. Herewith a ranking of cool animals and their drippy colleagues:

COOLEST ANIMALS

1. wolf
2. grizzly bear
3. tiger
   panther (black)
4. panther (any other color)
5. wolverine

LEAST COOL ANIMALS

1. pig
2. sheep/goat
3. cow
4. any rodent (except Templeton the rat from *Charlotte's Web*, who is cool)
5. cat

In short, the coolest animals are (a) wild and (b) carnivorous. What self-respecting animal is content to hang around a barnyard when he could be out there surviving with the fittest? And further, what kind of wild animal, having found the courage to eschew the safety of domestication, sits around waiting for his dinner to blossom instead of tearing a snack from the hindquarters of a springbok? No question: The coolest animals are usually found licking their chops.

My father once told me a story about how his father, while wrestling in the Belgian Congo with a panther made of midnight, had prevailed by reaching down the panther's throat and turning him inside out. The story had a wild, ferocious and God-bless-it carnivorous quality that has, in moments when the world threatens to declaw, been an adrenal call, a reminder of the undiminished that is the province of any father worth the job title.

STORY COOL

THE CONFESSIONS OF SCHEHERA-DAD

The ability to tell a story is about the coolest thing there is. Consider the idea of just plain making something up, putting something in a spot where there had been nothing. Consequently, among the paternal pleasures to which I most looked forward in the months before Joshua was born was the privilege of telling him stories. Each evening before commending him to sleep—so went the fantasy—I would fill his room with grand tales of treasure and jungle boys, born of Stevenson and Kipling, swashbuckling yet tenderhearted epics that he would surely pass on twenty-five years hence to his children.

Well, it hasn't worked out exactly as I'd planned. In fact, I'm a narrative nebbish. No matter where I start the stories I tell my kids, they always end in the same I-just-can't-help-it place. They always end up with the dancing squirrels.

They can begin on a distant star, in a supermarket, at the circus, inside a pumpkin, no matter. They always end up—without my permission—out of control in the same

PETERS DAY 0/1984

spooky moonlit glade with squirrels, a group of furry druids, holding paws and dancing in a heathen circle. Oh, sometimes there is an occasional minor variation. Sometimes they are beavers or chipmunks or even baby gophers. But deep down, beneath all the speciation, they're the same squirrels. It's gotten to the point where Josh can see them coming. "This isn't going to be about the squirrels, is it, Daddy?" he'll ask, a four-year-old diplomat trying to make it clear that he would prefer another climax. "No, Joshie," I'll say confidently, unfolding a tale of a sailor boy who saves his brother, swims with fish and flies his boat in the air. But you can be sure once he lands his boat the little sailor boy will peek out from behind a tree and see—not a fairy building a mushroom, not a little girl hiding in a cave of toys, not an elf painting the leaves of an oak tree—but a handful of creatures from the rodent family in the middle of a do-si-do.

In spite of my redundant failure Josh remains steadfast. He'll cuddle up next to me and say, "Tell me a story, Daddy." But my moment of delight in his hopefulness quickly gives way to panic when he adds, "Tell me a *new* story, Daddy. One you've never told me before." He's still waiting to hear one worth repeating, you see.

"Okay, Josh," I say, starting to riffle through my suddenly empty mental file. "Once upon a time . . ."

"Daddy, many stories begin once upon a time . . ."

"That's right, pal. Once upon a time . . ." Already repeating myself, stretching out single-syllable words in a pathetic hope that inspiration will descend. But there is nothing, and I mean nothing, in my mind. I have achieved the blankness of a Zen master.

"Once upon a time . . ."

"You already said that, Daddy."

"I know, Joshie," said tersely. "Once upon a time there was a . . . a . . . a . . ."

"A what, Daddy?"

Frantic glances around the room. A what? A couch? A table? A beer mug? A copy of *The New Republic*?

"Once upon a time there was a . . . a . . . a . . . a boy, that's it, a boy," actually said with satisfaction that I had pulled it out of the fire.

"A boy, Daddy?" he says as though sure I can't mean *a boy*, otherwise I wouldn't have taken so long to come up with it.

"Yes, a boy, a boy named . . . a boy named . . . named . . ."

"I hope he's not named Joshie," says my son, I believe without guile, reading my mind. "I don't like stories with boys named Joshie. I'm Joshie."

"No, no, no, of course he's not named Joshie," I

lie, as though shocked that he could underestimate me so.

"A boy named...named..." My computer program has been purged of every single male proper name I have ever heard. "Named...named...Henry, yes, Henry, that's his name, Henry," said with relief and as though the story is over.

"Henry?"

"Yes, Henry," I say defensively. "And not only that, he lived in the bottom of a tree," I expand, feeling rather more fecund than Homer himself.

"A boy who lived in the bottom of a tree?" he says skeptically.

"Yes, Josh," I say, holding my temper. "Yeah," I think, "wanna make something of it?"

And so on and so on...

I've tried everything. I've tried stealing from the masters. For about a week I managed to convince myself that my Steven Small, a mouse who lived with a nice family on Fifth Avenue, was like E. B. White's Stuart Little only insofar as they were both urban mice. Finally I went to my friend Jim, who is famous for the stories he tells his children. "Kids don't remember the plot," he said. "They just remember the details, the fact that Belinda has a tri-cornered hat that was robin's-egg blue. It's not the destination," he continued, playing the guru's role for all it was worth, "it's the journey."

The night after I spoke to Jim I had a momentary cause for hope. I started a story about a little girl who flew on the back of a butterfly; Josh seemed interested. Indeed, he actually looked up at me as though making sure that some guy who knew how to tell a story hadn't taken over my body. But that glance did it. Like the rookie pitcher who realizes there are two gone in the seventh and nobody's got a hit, I couldn't stand the pressure of success. I collapsed in a pathetic conclusion starring a family of black-footed ferrets in a wrestling tournament. Josh actually patted me reassuringly as he said good night.

I despair of ever being any good at that which I once imagined would be a piece of cake. I can only hope that the future won't also prove me wrong about the hours we'll spend hurling a grass-slicked baseball as evening comes. However, Josh is learning to read and so he has his own access to magic. As for me, though I'll never be confused with Scheherazade, I have learned a few hard lessons. Herewith, the bitter fruits of my misadventures offered so that others might be spared the ignominies I have endured.

THE THREE MOST COMMON PATERNAL STORYTELLING MISTAKES

The Moniker Fallacy

This mistake, christening characters with fruity names, calling a wonder horse Jupiter Esmeralda, reveals a fundamental weakness. Kids know that daddies rely on fancy names when they're trying to camouflage a second-rate story. In a good story a horse is named Buck or Old Joe (a mare is Belle). A squirrel is Graytail or Sam; under no circumstances is he Mr. Treeleaper.

The Aquarian Fallacy

This mistake, insisting that stories have no violence, is made most often by daddies of the sixties generation. Daddies who remember their number in the draft lottery tell stories about King Lettuce and King Cabbage, who, overcome by brotherhood during the hootenanny they cosponsored, decide to give up the idea of the nation-state and become one big Happy Land of Salad. The fact is, kids like violent things. Evidence: Those guys who wrote all those fairy tales weren't the Brothers Sweetness and Light. The battle of Antietam isn't a good idea, but a story without some kind of threat—be it a fire-breathing dragon who may ravage the land or a mere honey shortage—is a waste of time.

The Abracadabra Fallacy

This mistake, telling stories with too much magic, is made by daddies who have no idea where they're going with a story. So when they get stuck, they are reduced to poofety-poofety-poof, turning a troubled little tugboat into the maître d' at a cat and dog restaurant. Just when the child gets interested in whether the tugboat will ever find his sister—presto!—what used to be a brave little boat is serving quiche to a St. Bernard. Some magic is required, but too much magic, born of desperation, isn't storytelling at all. It's nonsense. Daddy Cool Rule of Thumb: *At least half the characters should finish the story in the same species in which they started.*

HOW TO TELL A COOL STORY

It is, of course, easier to say what not to do than to outline the elements of a good story. Also keep in mind that not all cool stories are good stories. Often kids will hate stories that are perfectly cool, preferring some goony little tale about a smiling rabbit. But your mental health is at stake here. So here are the facts about cool stories.

All cool stories are about one of three things:

1. The unambiguous triumph of good over evil

2. The unambiguous triumph of the motivated under-dog over a disdainful establishment

3. The rueful sadness of impossible love

An Example of Category 1

Black Bart Rabbit rolls into town and starts stealing everybody's lettuce. He's spoiling for a fight with the sheriff—a tall drink of rabbit, Gary Cooper-type, who doesn't think a fella's gotta carry a gun to be strong. At high noon, with the whole town peering out from behind shutters, Black Bart and the sheriff, who's going to marry a Grace Kelly-type rabbit later that day, face each other down. The sheriff convinces Bart that unless he changes his ways there's nothin' in this town for him. As Bart is about to draw on the sheriff, he suddenly sees the error of his ways and allows how perhaps violence is never the answer to a craving for roughage.

An Example of Category 2

A monosyllabic Italian rabbit who works in a meat-packing plant in Philly has a dream of being the champ. He trains in complete obscurity using sides of beef as a heavy bag. Driven by fierce desire and his love for his trainer, a Burgess Meredith-type rabbit, and Stella, the mousy rabbit girlfriend, he survives a bloodbath of a championship fight, eventually knocking out a Muhammad Ali-type rabbit against whom the experts didn't give him a prayer.

An Example of Category 3

Time: World War II. An American rabbit named Ric, who has been a few places and seen a few things, runs a club in Casablanca. One night, of all the gin joints in all the world she, Ilsa, a rabbit of Ingrid Bergmanesque beauty and style, walks in with her husband, a great Resistance Rabbit, whose character and commitment make a mockery of the merely lustful passion that Ric and Ilsa shared some years ago in Paris. Ilsa imagines that their romance can, indeed, must, be saved, but Ric, sensing her attachment to her heroic husband rabbit, tells her that although they'll always have Paris, she belongs with Resistance Rabbit and further that the problems of two rabbits don't amount to a hill of beans in this world. She flies reluctantly away from a fog-shrouded airport, leaving Ric to the consolation of charming cynical gendarme-rabbit, who knows that Ric isn't the tough bunny most of Morocco thinks he is.

In addition to falling into one of these three categories cool stories often feature:

1. Superlative characters—the world's *smallest* bug, the world's *fastest* snake, the world's *most garrulous* pig, the world's *shyest* shark, the world's most something. A cartoony quality, especially as far as minor characters are concerned, is vital. Focusing on extremes of one sort or another sends the subliminal message that the world ain't all that complex, a guy's either very something or he's not. Of course, this message isn't true, but it is cool.

2. A journey—preferably up or down a river à la *Huck Finn* or *The Heart of Darkness*. In a pinch a hegira across a desert or over a mountain range will do. The destination—be it home to Mommy Mouse or an assignation with the churlish Mistah Kurtz—must be mentioned early and repeated throughout. This device— used by storytellers from Homer to Aunt Eileen—

gives a story direction and can be used to good effect by fathers who are especially bad at plot.

3. A dramatic cinematic climax. Cool stories must always end with a bang—a great fire, a squirrel riding off into a Monument Valley sunset apparently in search of a better life. Cool stories promise freedom—often through heading west. However, cool stories never end with "happily ever after." They can end happily, of course, but they can't even make promises about tomorrow, not to mention ever after.

ONE LAST PIECE OF ADVICE

Invent recurring characters. Everybody likes soap operas featuring characters in whom we have a long-standing interest. My nieces, Katie and Annie Jamieson, clamor for the Bitsy (a bunny) and Henry (a bear) stories their parents have made family classics. Remember, these are legends you're hoping to pass from generation to generation. Some of them should begin with you. I like to imagine that when Katie and Annie and Molly are all grown-up and fine, and hear the name Henry, they'll get a flash of their daddy's whiskers at 7 P.M.

NOT AN EXCUSE, JUST AN EXPLANATION

Every time I think I've come to terms with my storytelling incompetence I find myself inventing some marvelous justification for my futility. But of all my excuses none makes me look better than my most recent, which goes as follows: I'm a lousy storyteller because Josh's reality—his taste,

his scent, the texture of his skin, the shiver of his brain—
makes anything artificial seem just that. I'm a bad storyteller because he, and his sister, Rebecca, green-eyed and
wild behind him, are the only stories I can imagine.

GROOMING **C**OOL

HOW TO
FIND YOUR CLOTHES

Rare is the man who doesn't have some sartorial style. Oh, the styles vary greatly—from the pocket-square dandy to the I've-got-a-few-things-more-important-than-clothes-on-my-mind schlump. Some spend time on the package; others take careful pride in neglecting it. But nine out of ten guys present themselves to the world, invite the world to make its guesses about us based—at least in part—on whether we're denim or linen, clean-shaven burger or swarthy knave.

Of all the changes—psychological and otherwise—wrought by fatherhood, the devastation of our groomed selves is among the most dramatic. Once the kids arrive, you stop *presenting* yourself to the world and start hoping the world's not looking.

FETERS DATOPRCT

THE RAZOR'S HEDGE: DEALING WITH THE ONE O'CLOCK SHADOW

Before men have children, there are times when shaving seems a burden, a daily obligation of nick and staunch. But once the kids get here, we look back nostalgically at the quiet time it was—we recall a delicious solitudinous male ritual, the very stuff of fresh starts. Before we were fathers we shaved at 7 A.M. After we become fathers the only time we have nine minutes for ablutions is midnight. Consequently what is for guys without children a five o'clock shadow shows up on fathers around noon. 'Long about lunchtime you'll start reminding people of their seedy Uncle Bob. There's just flat no way to prevent it; just go with it.

With one o'clock shadow you've got only two choices. You can act like (1) a conventional guy who forgot to shave or (2) a desperado. This is, of course, no choice at all. Go with desperado.

Desperado Scenario 1

You are sure that the woman at the dry cleaner is thinking to herself, "Gee, I hope that nice Mr. Gleason hasn't taken to drink, like my seedy Uncle Bob." Your only hope for keeping her respect is to eschew standard dry-cleaning gab ("The glen-plaid three-piece has a stain on the seat") for a salutation with Desperado Style like "Helluva day, isn't it, doll? Tastes like a good day to die."

Desperado Scenario 2

You sense that your customer is resisting your sales pitch because he has a hunch that any guy who looks like his seedy Uncle Bob can't be trusted to deliver service on desktop units. He says, "You know, you remind me of my mother's brother, Robert." Don't take the bait. Just rub your hand over your chin as though you're just dying for a good shave and say, as though there's nobody else in the room, "I tell you I'm not going back there without an order—at least not alive."

The point is to act like a guy who's run out of options. It ain't Winston Churchill but it's better than Ray Milland in *Lost Weekend*.

WARDROBE WORRIES: OF MIXING AND MATCHING

Another real wardrobe downside of paternity is that you'll find yourself wearing strange combinations of clothes. Whereas you used to get dressed deliberately, choosing a shirt that made sense with the pants, now you get dressed in a hurry. You've got to get outside before the children can sell the car to the mailman. So you grope, in a drowsy panic, into your closet and two times out of three will find yourself decked out in sweatpants, a cummerbund and a dickey.

The best defense is to buy only clothes that look presentable when worn together. In other words, your closet must not be home to olive slacks *and* a kelly-green golf shirt. If they're both in there, the imp of the perverse will guide your morning hand to them. So remember the fundamental rule: *The better looking a garment, the fewer things you can wear with it*. Those brown tweed slacks with the subtle blue flecks are too demanding to be part of a father's wardrobe. Buy lots of black, white, gray, and never—repeat, never—buy anything that is a color you can't describe with one word. Particularly risky are colors knows as *teal* and *aubergine*.

Downside: These rules make it pretty tough to look like something out of *GQ*.

Upside: They make it equally tough to look like something out of *Psychotic Weekly*.

AND SO TO BED: OF NAKEDNESS AND NIGHTGOWNS

About nocturnal attire there is a hard-and-fast rule. *Fathers sleep in their underwear.* Consider the alternatives:

PAJAMAS: These are for guys playing opposite Mary Astor.

NIGHTGOWNS: These are for guys who admire Thomas Jefferson too much.

NAKED: Ask yourself—Lizzie wakes up screaming with night visions and gets an eyeful of *Homo paternitas* cunningly backlit by the hall light. No way.

No, none of these will do. Cool fathers sleep in their underwear. A white T-shirt (with sleeves) and boxer shorts— either blue, white, plaid, or bearing a Drexel Burnham logo.

On the Temptation of Matching Clothes

Never wear clothes that match your children's clothes. Believe me, you'll be tempted. You'll be so enthused about that day at Jimbo's Chutes 'n' Ladders that you'll find yourself paying $18.50 for two T-shirts featuring Jimbo himself splashing down the log flume. The instinct— the spirit of remembrance, of legend-making—is good. But the technique is cheap. There is something elementally sad about a grown man in a kid's shirt. Remember: *One of you is the father, the other the child.*

WHAT THE **B**IG **G**UY **K**NOWS **A**BOUT **B**EING **S**OMEBODY'S **F**ATHER

Moses Malone is among the leading rebounders in the history of the NBA. As of this writing he has grabbed the ball off the rim 14,802 times. He who would thrive as daddy might consider the Malone style.

Moses will get the ball down low, spin, lunge toward the hoop, throw up an absolute brick that clangs artlessly off the rim. Then he'll go strongly, stolidly after the ball, as though it's his, as though he's the only guy on the court, as though the "shot" he just took was intended to set him up for the rebound. He'll grab the ball, fire it toward the basket again, watch it thwomp off the glass and reclaim it once more before stuffing it violently, finally, through the defenseless basket.

The paternal lesson of Malone is simple relentlessness. The man is a horse. The man has a huge powerful body. But more important, he's got a huge powerful will. He simply keeps after it.

The Washington Bullets don't pay him to shoot three-

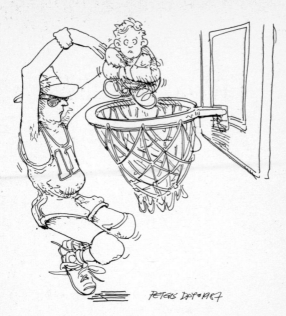

PETERS DAY 1987

pointers. They don't pay him to lead the league in assists.
They pay him to keep after it. That's his job.

For anybody—man or woman—trying to be a decent
parent, Moses taking the ball to the glass is a useful
image. Consider: It's 9:30 P.M. The kids are still awake.
They want a glass of water, Daddy. There's a monster in
the closet, Daddy. They've scattered a box of Band-Aids
around the house ("Just like Hansel did, Daddy, to find his
way home"). You're straining to reach the corn muffin
under the couch. Everywhere you turn is an obligation of
some sort, sometimes trivial, sometimes grand. Everywhere is a demand that you do your job. And you're tired.
S-o-o-o-o-o tired.

Think of each daddy task as the final offensive rebound,
the one before the buzzer-beating dunk. Turn off your
mind, turn on your will. Get like Moses.

GENDER **C**OOL

OF TESTOSTERONE AND SLEEPING BEAUTY

My own most revealing experience with gender cool took place with my son, Josh, in a toy store. He zoomed through the store, trying to decide what toy he should bring home, bouncing from the water pistols to the Wuzzles earmuffs. Finally, when he had it narrowed down to two toys, he asked me to help him choose.

"Which do you think we should get, Daddy?" he said, holding out a Smurf alphabet sketching pad and a Sleeping Beauty makeup kit. Though before this moment I imagined myself pretty calm about gender roles (after all, in the sixties I had actually worn clogs in public), the idea of my son mastering retractable lip gloss and primping in front of the hand-held mirror was too much for me. All of my male-bonding fantasies—the camping trips, the ball games—were swamped by the thought of my boy in a jumper.

I pretended to labor over the decision, looking at each toy carefully, pointing out that the Smurf pad had many different colors of paper and every letter in the whole wide world, before saying I thought it was the better choice. He

looked at me as though his question had been a test. I knew in an instant I had made a mistake. "Naw," he said, heaving the Smurf pad over his shoulder, "this is the funnest, Daddy." With that he held the Sleeping Beauty makeup kit over his head as though he were showing the crowd the Stanley Cup and continued, "I can be Sleeping Beauty," he whispered, "and you can be the Wicked Queen." Not exactly Butch and Sundance, I thought. With that, he batted his eyelashes at me and headed for the cashier, visions, I'm sure, of Georgette Klinger in his head.

Looking back, I'm sure he would have chosen the pad if I had chosen the makeup kit. If I had, I could have traded countless hours spent squawking "Mirror, mirror on the wall" in a Wicked Queen voice (Josh confused Sleeping Beauty with Snow White) for quiet times teaching him the glories of a few Smurf words like *love, hope, grace* and *pizza.* No two ways about it—my response to his question was anything but cool. Uptight? Yes. Gender-anxious? You bet. Cool? Not even vaguely.

GENDER COOL QUIZ I

Your four-year-old son tells you he wishes he were a girl. What should you do?

1. Say, "Oh no you don't, boyo, believe me. It's no bargain being a girl."

2. Cuff him playfully on the back of the head while saying in an effeminate voice, "Oh, little Roy wants to be a girl, does he?"

3. Say, "Do you really, Roy? I used to wish I were a girl when I was your age."

4. Ignore it.

Answer Analysis

1. I need to believe nobody could possibly choose this answer.

2. Making fun of your son is a perfectly reasonable option if you prefer that he keep all his thoughts to himself the rest of his days.

3. Saying you used to wish you were a girl is tempting but it's an obvious attempt to make him think he's normal. He'll know you're just saying it to assure him he's not a sicko, which he will therefore become convinced he is.

4. This is the cool answer.

QUIZ II

Your six-year-old daughter says girls can't be doctors. You should:

1. Say, "I'm afraid you're wrong, Hester. Ever since the feminist movement more and more doctors are, sad to say, female."

2. Grab her by the shoulders, shake her harshly, look her square in the eyes and say, "You listen to me, woman-child. You are an eagle and eagles can fly."

3. Say, "You're wrong, doll, this is America."

Answer Analysis

Some would argue that answer 2 is politically correct and therefore acceptable. But cool guys don't refer to children as eagles. The Daddy Cool answer is 3. Cool guys are pluralists and think everybody—including dames—oughta do whatever the hell they wanna do. They also think this is the right country in which to do it.

SCHOOL COOL

OF BIG RICHARD AND THOSE LITTLE CHAIRS

It was two days after our Rebecca was born and Josh's first day at nursery school. Jody and the girl were still in the hospital, so I dressed Josh up in his shining morning face and we were suddenly in a school lobby awash with children. It occurred to me that my daughter had just arrived but my son—all thirty-one, skinny, red-headed pounds of him—was taking off.

We milled around, trying to figure out where Miss Weinstein's class was gathering. He was interested, tempted by the chaos, yet unsure of anything that didn't include Mommy or Daddy. As we stood waiting for the teacher to appear, he spotted a group of boys—clearly bigger, more boy-like than Josh—playing with what looked like a space shuttle. "Can I play with those boys, Daddy?" he said. "Sure," I said, "just go say hello." He scooted over and said, "Hello, my name is Josh O'Neill. Can I play with you?" The other boys just looked at him and continued vrooming their ship through the air, as though asking somebody if you could play with them was strictly three-year-old stuff.

Josh sat in their midst, clearly pleased that life should feature such a band of boys. After a few minutes, when he got up and walked back to me, the largest of the boys peeled off and followed him.

"He's just a baby. He wears diapers," said Mussolini Jr. over his shoulder to his pals, gesturing with his chin toward Josh. He was the spirit of the Hun, the gratuitously violent urge that is among our burdens. I was tempted to pop this five-year-old in the kisser. As two of his henchmen drifted over to him, Josh moved back against me and felt his backside, clearly checking to see if he was indeed wearing a diaper, and then he looked up at me as though for encouragement. With a quiver in his voice he looked into the dull eyes of this bigger, aggressive, hostile Attila of a child, and said, "I only wear diapers in the car." It was neither a denial nor an admission. It was, quite simply, the truth—a confession made necessary not because he was anything less than manly when it came to self-control, but because his father was stupid about unscheduled stops. It was, to be sure, a far more civil response than this thug deserved. The plain-old liberating, straight-in-the-eye truth. No tears, no turning to Daddy for protection. Just the facts. I remember thinking that if his life went according to plan, he might never have to be braver than he had just been.

Then one of the two lieutenants flanking the Ancestral Enemy, apparently now confused because his daddy made him wear diapers in the car too, looked at his leader, not with the moronic admiration of ten seconds ago, but with the shimmer of a still-possible person who had, suddenly and forever, seen through the allure of the jackboot. He turned and walked away, Josh looked up at me, and in a moment Stalin Jr. and his other goon were gone as well. Suddenly, without actually making a decision, I walked Josh toward the door, unready for the boy to go to school. I remember

thinking that the world—even this sweet decent school—
was, compared with him, a hopeless vulgarity.

I remember thinking that I wasn't ready to commend my
son into the hands of people who knew none of the
following things:

1. That Tooney's couch, the blue one, was named by
   Josh after the man who reupholstered it
2. What a racoon blanket was
3. That "Orange Herbert" was a kind of ice cream
4. That a weasel was something you paint on

The world didn't know any of the secrets that were the
very stuff of our home, the messages that, taken together,
made the three (now four) of us different from anything
that had ever happened anywhere before. As I walked with
the boy out the door I was in thrall to our romance,
unprepared to go public with our act.

When kids arrive at school age, you face a whole new
series of challenges to your cool. After all, it's the first
time you share your children with the world. Until you
sign them up for something communal, for all the world
knows you could be teaching them to speak in Olde
English. But with the coming of academia you've got to at
least tip your hat to out there. No question, when they start
school they stop being just yours and start belonging to the
ages. I remember the first time Josh came home from
kindergarten telling me all about the disinformation some
guy named Richard, who was "just five, but, big, Daddy," was spreading around P.S. 6. From then on I found
myself explaining lots of stuff. I have a vivid memory of
telling Josh that there were still a few things I knew more
about than Richard.

Though the psychological stresses of letting go are
considerable, they are nothing compared with the raft of

new and humiliating situations in which school will put you. Some survival tips for three of the most troubling.

QUIZ:
HOW TO SURVIVE THOSE
LITTLE CHAIRS

Almost every school in America has parents' orientation night, the night when twenty-six-year-old teachers named Jennie invite all the dads and moms to make themselves comfortable on those tiny little painted chairs from the Thumbelina collection. On getting the invitation you should:

1. Sit down and lean back, resting your hands on the floor behind the chair and stretching your legs out in front of you in the manner of Henry Fonda as young Mr. Lincoln.

2. Sit primly with your knees drawn up in front of you, your chin resting, Gidget-like, on top of them.

3. Stand next to the chair and put one foot up on it, leaning forward, resting your forearm intently on your thigh in the manner of General Ridgway planning a flanking action.

Answer Analysis

None of these options is acceptable. Though I've seen guys get away with number 3, it's a long shot. Don't go near that chair. Just don't do it. Put it in your pocket. Scratch your back with it. Pin it to your lapel. If you have to, pick it up, break it to pieces over the sand table. I don't care. Just don't sit on it. If you do you'll feel diminished for the rest of your life.

HOW TO CARRY A STRAWBERRY SHORTCAKE LUNCH BOX

Believe me, every morning Daddy gets to carry the lunch box to school. Seth will be overburdened with much more prized possessions, including the Skeletor helmet and the Ghostbuster gun. Now, your basic black (or silver) tunnel-shaped construction-worker lunch box is cool. Hell, guys who carry those built the World Trade Center. But those rectangular jobs featuring Pebbles and Bam-Bam, those are a different story; those are bad news. There's not much you can do to minimize the damage, but there is one small, sometimes useful, trick.

Don't carry it by the handle. Holding a cartoon lunch box by the handle somehow alters your gait—from macho shamble into cheerful bounce. You'll find yourself walking like sixties guys who wore earth shoes. Not good. So, eschew convenience and grab the box itself with your whole hand, smothering the chirpy clicking handle against the top of it. This will suggest that the handle is a damn nuisance to a guy with mitts like yours, who's most at home hefting two-by-fours. Also, once in a while casually hold the lunch box at arm's length over your head or at your side, in a manner of Kareem in the low post teasing his competition with the tiny ball.

How to Behave
at a Parent-Teacher Conference

My father did the parent-teacher conference perfectly. He would sit down after thanking Miss Crabtree for being one of America's unexalted heroes. Then he would listen with pleasure as she said what an honor it was to have a child such as me or Nancy or Kevin or Kathy or Eileen or Tim or Mary in her class.

He would nod with pride as she cataloged our achievements in math, in reading, in civics, in art. But then, as her tone of voice changed and she began her segue into "however," he would stand briskly up, thank her once again for doing God's work with such vigor and excuse himself politely. In brief, my father would bask in all the good stuff, but demur on the nickel-and-dime downside.

I'm not sure this was wise. But, boy, was it cool. After all, what kind of guy just sits and listens while his pal takes it in the neck?

HOW TO
ARRANGE QUADRUPLE
JUMPS

Fathers and games are an age-old match. Chess, for example, was invented by an ancient and desperate Sumerian father who hoped that getting the kids engaged in its meditative intricacies might give him a chance to floss. Further, though it's well known that Parcheesi is an antique Pakistani game, few realize that Chutes & Ladders, Candyland, Clue and Twister, even the Wuzzles Treasure Game, are all modern versions of games originally developed by fathers who were just plain pooped.

HOW TO PLAY GAMES
WITH THE KIDS

The fundamental cool rule about playing games with kids is simple: *Lose. Always lose.* Shut up. *Just lose.*
Here's how:

Candyland

Because this game is complete luck, unless you take some precautions you'll win half the time. So if you're approaching the Candy Castle, just pretend the next card you draw is Gumdrop Mountain, which sends your Gingerbread man all the way back to the start. Now, your daughter may be surprised because she's a card-counter and is sure that Gumdrop Mountain was chosen nine cards ago. Fear not. Her misgivings about the truth will give way to her competitive glee at the sight of your green cookie-cutter figure taking the Long March back, back, hopelessly back to Square One. You can also rely on the Molasses Swamp Technique. It is a mere thirteen squares from Candy Castle, and any daddy with ingenuity can not only manage in a pinch to land on it but also to palm any red card which might threaten to set him free.

Checkers: King Me Cool

Losing at checkers is a bit more complex because you can't lose unless your opponent has at least a minimal level of competence. The Daddy Cool trick is to make the required terrible move, then, the moment you take your finger off the checker, slap your palm woefully to your forehead and say, "Oh no, that leaves me wide open on the left for a quadruple jump that will lead to a king for you."

Oh, I know, I've heard all the arguments. The kids should learn to play fair. They should learn about rules. They should learn about gamesmanship. They should come to understand that winning isn't everything, that winning doesn't matter. Exactly. That's exactly why you have to lose all the time—to show them that winning doesn't matter. After all, your kids aren't stupid; they know you're losing on purpose. And they know you're doing it because you know they love to win. Unless you lose all the time the kids will think that winning does matter. Show me a man who doesn't always let his kids win, and I'll show you a man too hungry for victories.

GAMESMANSHIP AND HOME MAINTENANCE: THE MARY POPPINS THEORY

No father should ever forget Mary Poppins's words of wisdom: "In every job that must be done there is an element of fun. Find the fun and...snap! The job's a game." All fathers should give serious thought to trying out the following games:

1. The First Annual Smithson Family Fill-the-Wheelbarrow-With-Leaves Race

2. The Grand Empty-the-Junk-filled-Garage-in-Search-of-the-Chocolate-Bunny Game

3. The Vernal-Equinox-Scrub-the-Screens Water Festival

Children have enormous physical energy. If you can somehow—however briefly—tap into it by turning your chores into a game, you'll find yourself with twenty minutes to spend with the Tom Watson video on the short game. Of course you'll only get away with each fraud once. Kids have a way of sensing when something productive is being accomplished and so losing interest. Pick your spots.

POEM COOL

ON PATERNAL PENTAMETER

Granted: Our literature features thousands of great poems and songs for children. And it's cool to give the kids a taste of them all—from Stevenson's "Lamplighter" to Burl Ives's "Froggy Went a-Courtin'"—but a truly cool father occasionally ascends above tradition and comes up with a song or poem of his own.

Hopeless, you say? You're not a word man? You're lucky to *remember* "The Mouse Ran Up the Clock"? Coming up with something of your own is a bit of a reach? Not so, once you know the trick.

The key to paternal poetry is to aspire to unconventional rhymes. The key is to be a daddy who doesn't rhyme "fox" with "box" or "sox," but with the short form of Nova Scotia salmon, lox.

THE AMBITIOUS DADDY'S RYHMING GUIDE

WORD	CONVENTIONAL RHYME	COOL RHYME
bear	chair care hair	*mon père*

If you're merely content to rhyme "bear" with "chair" you'll end up with a pedestrian poem like, "There once was a bear/Who sat on a chair." Your four-year-old will be thinking, "No kidding, Dad, I suppose he slept in his lair too." But if you start with "bear" and have to get to "*mon père*," the ambition of that transit will commend your brain to the unusual. Consider:

There once was a little brown bear
Lived in Lille, called his daddy mon père.

That's a couplet to be proud of. It has detail and suggests everything from the romance of France to the astonishing variety of human language.

WORD	CONVENTIONAL RHYME	COOL RHYME
cow	sow	Mao
	wow	
	now	

A daddy with no imagination would versify:

There once was a brown and white cow,
Whose best friend was Sally the Sow.

A poetically cool father would do much better:

There once was a brown and white cow,
Who didn't say moo but said Mao.

The first couplet doesn't launch you into a poem. It gives you no momentum, no plot line, no engine for your epic. The second cool couplet, by demanding the ingenuity to get from "cow" to "Mao," inherits narrative drive. It's clearly the start of something Homeric, which can, depending on your political preference, be about the threat of communism to freedom everywhere or about the eventual and much-to-be-desired withering away of the industrial state in favor of a people's republic.

On the Necessity of "Casey at the Bat"

There is only one poem to which every American child must—at an early age—be exposed: "Casey at the Bat." Those who hear it early cannot help but turn out to be fine people. Those who don't will have a tougher time. It is, in short, the coolest poem ever written. Here are three reasons why:

1. It rhymes "saw what had occurred" with "Flynn a-huggin' third."

2. It captures—in the drawn-out account of Casey's penultimate at-bat—the delicious/painful moment of anticipation/dread that is at the heart of our national game and without an understanding of which no child of either gender can have a decent American life.

3. And most important, it celebrates style, even in failure. Casey's arrogant swagger—his marvelous pridefulness—is undiminished by strike one, two or three. There may be no joy in Mudville but the human drama is everywhere afoot. We are, in Yeats's phrase, bred to a harder thing than triumph. That fake-doleful ending

   > ...*somewhere men are laughing and somewhere children shout,*
   > *But there is no joy in Mudville—mighty Casey has struck out.*

   couldn't be less sad. Ah yes, says the poem to the child, he failed, but with extravagant style.

ON JOHN KEATS AND POETIC FEATS

Thousands of poets have spent careers trying to define the creative sensibility. Though it's hard to imagine what any guy who had the time to write "Ode on a Grecian Urn" could possibly have to teach a guy who rhymes "verse" with "Smurfs," the young aesthete John Keats, who died of sensitivity at age twenty-six, came up with a definition of the poet which can inspire all fathers through the chaos that children finally are. Keats held that the real poet had "negative capability," defined as the ability to be in "uncertainties, mysteries, doubts without any irritable reaching after fact and reason."

In other words, the real poet doesn't get bent out of shape just because there's yogurt on the wall and somebody small is accusing her brother of hitting her with an invisible hammer. After all, what kind of guy comes apart just because his house does?

One hundred years after Keats passed on, his soulmate Wallace Stevens defined a poet as a "connoisseur of chaos," which is a perfect way for any daddy who would survive the darkest hours to think of himself. You've got to love the madness. "With a great poet," wrote Keats, "the sensing of Beauty overcomes every other consideration, or rather obliterates all consideration." Amid the storm, there is only the color of your son's hair.

Get like Keats and his buddies.

FIX-IT **C**OOL

OF TREE HOUSES AND DADDY'S TOOLS

Being handy, being good with things—cars, tools, pipes, machines, devices of all sorts—is cool. Mothers and kids just love daddies who can whip up a playhouse between dessert and coffee. We like to imagine ourselves at home with ratchet wrenches, undaunted by ripsaws, finely tuned to the sound of transmission trouble. But these days many of us have been so estranged from our survival instincts that a guy is considered handy if he knows who to call.

For those of us mired in ineffectuality, learning the art of masonry just isn't in the cards. But there is one chance that we can allow our children to see us as the fixer-uppers of the world.

The trick is to accentuate the positive. The trick is to get them when they're young. When the children are small and impressionable, make a big deal out of all the things you actually *can* do—like tying your shoes, and putting the cap on the toothpaste.

PETERS DAY•1987

HOW TO CHANGE A FUSE

Imagine the scene. For a moment your house is domestic tranquillity itself. The kids are watching *101 Dalmatians* on the VCR. Your wife is talking to her brother on the phone. You're riffling through the baseball encyclopedia in pursuit of the most triples in a season by a third baseman of Italian descent. The dishwasher is sloshing, stereo crooning—your electrical village is thrumming away—when suddenly everything stops. *101 Dalmatians* aborts to juvenile lament. The stereo fades to quiet. The dishwasher settles for midcycle plink. It's dark, dark, I mean dark. There is an instant of huge silence and then the kids—ages five, three and fifteen months—come surging round the corner through the dark, landing in your lap.

Step One: Say, "It's all right, kids. Don't worry. Daddy will fix it." Notice that you don't say, *"We'll* have it fixed in a jiffy," nor do you say, *"I'll* fix it." No, the operative word here is "Daddy." You want the kids to associate the word "Daddy" with the word *"fix."*

Step Two: Go to the kitchen and get two candles. Light one and put it on the dining room table. Candle glow adds to the drama of just about anything. Subliminally the kids will think you're something like the Wizard of Oz.

Step Three: Light the other candle, say, "I'll get *my* fuses," and disappear with flame into the storage closet. Once in there, don't just pick up the fuses from the shelf. Rather, make enough noise to suggest that you're doing something rather more druidical, something about which only daddies could possibly know. Notice again a key word. Don't say, "I'll get *the* fuses," or "I'll get *some* fuses." That suggests that someone who was not their father could handle this situation. No, the key word is "my."

Step Four: Walk past the children on the way to the basement and make sure that the candle illuminates your face. Say nothing.

Step Five: As you're about to give the final decisive twist to the new fuse, shout, "Let there be light," from the basement. This phrase has mythic clout—even if your kids haven't read Genesis. Indeed, it may be even better if they're not familiar with the reference. Once they come upon it in school, they'll think God is imitating Daddy. *In general, whenever possible, link yourself with making out of darkness light.*

The general lessons here can be applied to any number of mundane paternal maintenance tasks—changing a light bulb, installing batteries in a remote-control robot, sucking up Sugar Smacks with a Dustbuster. Kids are easily impressed. Allow your children to reminisce about the jungle gym you never actually built, about that summer you installed central air. Allow them to imagine that life is a can-do proposition.

NICKNAME COOL

OF BUBBA AND BOYO

Certain nicknames for children are cool. Others aren't.

COOL NICKNAMES FOR BOYS	UNCOOL NICKNAMES FOR BOYS
Hoss	Trip
Bubba	Sweetlips
Pally	Mister Muscles
Boyo	Bigfoot
Boychik	Binky
Babe	Mel

The general rule is that a nickname for a son is only as cool as it is likely to come out of the mouth of an SEC football coach or of a guy named Moe whose partner Solly died last June.

COOL NICKNAMES FOR GIRLS	UNCOOL NICKNAMES FOR GIRLS
Girl	Sunshine
Face	Light of My Life
Doll	Muffin

COOL NICKNAMES FOR GIRLS	UNCOOL NICKNAMES FOR GIRLS
Babe	Little Lady
Slats	Mel

The general rule here is that a nickname for a daughter is only as cool as it is likely to come out of the mouth of a gangster. No question, there is sexism afoot here. After all, there ain't much less cool than not knowing the difference between a mug and a real tomato.

SEX **C**OOL

HOW TO MAKE LOVE TO THEIR MOTHER

There are two good things about sex before you have children. One, you can plan it and two, you don't have to.

But once you have children, sex of either kind—lustfully anticipated or suddenly there—becomes a memory. You can say good-bye to the long languorous post-film date where you spend two hours trying to turn each other inside out. And you can forget the ravenous improvisational encounter in the den. Once you're a parent, sex of any kind is a real long shot—one of the children is always clinging to your leg.

There is an upside to this. Before having children, many couples report that their biggest sexual problem is agreeing that they're in the mood at the same time. This is no problem after kids arrive. Indeed, often the sexual deprivation of Mommy and Daddy is so great that on those rare occasions when the children are asleep at the same time, people who were moments ago doing a Miss Piggy jigsaw puzzle assault each other with the uninhibited abandon of

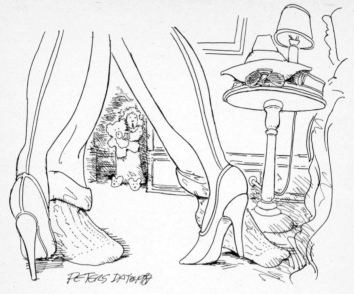

arctic wolves. Mood, schmood; the kids are asleep. When you're a parent, it's either right now or Flag Day.

Of course, the biggest threat to your sex life isn't the fact that the children turn all those summer-sun, fresh-linen afternoons, those old times of murmur and surge, into times of Play-Doh and squeal. The biggest threat is what they do to what used to be called your sex appeal. Consider their influence on just two of your primary sexual characteristics, your hair and your posture.

On Paternal Hair

Women have a thing about men's hair. In all those surveys of what women look for in a man, good hair ranks higher than everything but a nicely faded pair of jeans. Indeed, good hair is often the only difference between a cute guy and a guy who always looks sweaty. What do children do to your hair? First, once you have kids, you'll never again have a chance to comb it. But second, and more important, a kid riding on a grown man's shoulders tends to hang on by the hair. Four-year-old fists full of sand just don't do much for the coif. The fact is, most women can spot a daddy from his hairstyle—parted on both sides.

On Paternal Posture

A man's posture means a lot to his woman. It doesn't really matter what kind of body you have as long as you carry yourself with an easy shambling swagger, as long as you move like a guy who's at home on this particular planet. But fatherhood blows your posture right out of the water. Even if you've mastered the slightly pigeon-toed shuffle of the varsity athlete, children devastate your style. The truth is, it's near impossible to be cool on your hands and knees. It's tough to remind her of Claude Rains when you and your daughter have just won the crab-walking relay.

Once you're a father, you won't look or move anything like the stud-duck who once made her face warm. Consequently, if you're to have any chance to remain the object of her lust, you've got to work on a subliminal level. A few suggestions:

1. On occasion do a Bogart imitation. While gesturing with a jelly glass of wine toward her, say in no-matter-how-bad-as-long-as-it's-clearly-Bogey voice, "Here's lookin' at you, kid." I know this sounds like a cheap trick, but these are desperate times. Trust me.

2. Wear her father's after-shave. This is complex but not dumb. Better to smell like her father than like strained peas.

3. Whenever possible, wear shades. Sunglasses are not fatherly; they're cool. Alternately consider wearing a headband and denim jacket while strutting around the house singing "Born in the U.S.A."

4. Remind her of stories about the early days of your romance—that time you danced in the courtyard, your first kiss. If necessary, make up romantic things you did to win her heart. The goal is to remind her that you remain her Lancelot despite the oatmeal on your shoes.

Of course, even if you're able to convince your wife that you're still a hot ticket, paternal fatigue can be an obstacle to a vigorous sex life. Often by the time the children are asleep Mommy and Daddy can barely breathe—not to mention do the D. H. Lawrence skit.

But any successful creature adapts to its environment, husbands its resources. Parents must learn to have minimal sex, conserving their energy for the next onslaught of the children.

How to Have Sex Without Moving

Anybody can be sexy when they can move. After all, we've got an astonishing array of sexual tools. But suppose you can't move? Suppose your children have so deprived you of both sex and energy that you find yourself desperately wanting the former but afraid it just might kill you. Fear not. Daddy Cool can have sex without moving. Just trade in the spirit of thrust and grab, the images of piston and claw, for the spirit of yield and rub, the images of sponge and sponge. Lie down behind your wife in the manner of two spoons in a drawer, put your arms around her and go gently to sleep, dreaming about the days when you were young and vulgar.

Of course there will be times when you're nostalgic for the good-old-fashioned kind of sex. And so...

THE DISNEYLAND GAMBIT: AN EMERGENCY TECHNIQUE FOR BEING ALONE WITH YOUR WIFE

Tell the kids that you and Mommy are going into your room to plan a trip to Disneyland. Tell them you need privacy because you'll be calling hotels, mapping out a route, writing letters to Goofy and Mickey. Go big with the trip. Really sell the family adventure. But make it extremely clear that none of this will happen, that nobody in this family will get within a time zone of the Magic Kingdom, if Mommy and Daddy are disturbed in any way for the next half hour.

Now, you and your wife are going to have to renew acquaintance to the sound of your children singing "Hi-ho, hi-ho," but, I promise you, your privacy could not be safer if your bedroom had no door. Kids don't screw around with Disneyland.

Of course, the Disneyland Gambit is going to cost you. You've got to come across with the trip. So big deal. You go to the bank and get a Disneyland loan at three points over prime. You wanna make love to your wife or not? Remember, this technique is a one-shot. So don't waste it when you merely crave your wife unspeakably. Save it for the moment when you start to lose consciousness from sex debt.

ON THE ETHICS OF
CONTINUING TO MAKE LOVE WHEN
YOUR NEWBORN BABY WAKES
UP AND STARTS
TO CRY

Most psychologists claim that you do your baby no favor by picking him up the moment he starts to cry. Therefore, in theory, it shouldn't matter what you're doing as you ignore him. Still, watching a ball game seems somehow okay, but working your way through the Kama Sutra as your child screams, entertaining the to-him-plausible thought, "My God, they've left me here to die under a mobile playing 'The Farmer in the Dell,' " goes somehow over the line. The best wisdom—from mothers, fathers and child psychologists—on this question seems to be as follows:

Yes, your baby is a person. But so are Mommy and Daddy; they have needs too. So if you or your wife is within, say, two minutes of being a fully satisfied human being and therefore a better parent, you owe it to your child to, as Jane Fonda said in another context, go for the burn. If you're less highly evolved at the moment of first wail, turn on the tube and try not to be hostile to the best thing that ever happened to you.

DADDY COOL SEX TEST

You are making love to your wife in a way that no two people have ever previously made love—with more sweetness, ferocity and delight than ought to be possible in a world of matter. Suddenly from down the hall you hear your nine-month-old start to cry.

You:

1. Start to cry yourself.

2. Tell your wife the Petersons just bought a cat.

3. Say, "Damn, babe, that's Julie," and disingenously start to disengage, hoping she'll stop you.

Answer Analysis

1. This is wrong because cool guys don't cry. Period. End of discussion. Shut up . . . I said, shut up.

2. She'll know you're lying about the cat and come to share the conventional wisdom that all men are pigs interested in one thing and one thing only.

3. This is the right answer. If she thinks your father glands are working she may let her mother glands relax. A cool guy puts his kids' well-being before his own but he also puts his wife's well-being before his kids' convenience. So if you start to get up you win either way. In the unlikely event she lets you go, at least you get points as a good father. In the event you let her stop you from getting up, which she may well do given the fact that she wasn't sure she remembered how to do what you had just been doing, you're a great husband determined to stand by his woman.

A FINAL WORD

When all is said and done, the truth is, cool guys don't have sex. The Duke never did; neither did Cagney. They were too busy building a new land to be bothered with nookie. Sex is hot; it is most definitely not cool.

Joshua Cool

OF MAGIC AND THE REAL WORLD

Autumn, gold and smoke, winter in the wind, turning over wet leaves with three-year-old kicks, the boy park-bound with Daddy, made gabby by us together.

"Daddy, can I ask you something?" A trademark question, too polite, I imagine, prelude to something that's been on his mind.

"Sure, son, what is it?" indulging in the word "son."

"Daddy, is there such a thing as 'magic'?" he asks.

Josh thinks his question is about matter. Can things disappear? Reappear? Can rabbits emerge from empty hats? But his question isn't about matter at all, it's about optimism and hope. His question is about possibility.

A quick decision. Life needs no embellishment. The magician's skill at duplicity is marvel enough. And so..."Well, Joshie, that man at Sarah's party was doing terrific tricks. He's practiced very hard to be good at hiding things, at moving his hands quickly..."

"No, no, Daddy," he interrupts, "I know about magicians but I'm talking about *magic*. Is there such a thing as

magic?'' This last actually said with three-year-old italics.

(Why, of course, thank you, son of mine. Of course there is magic. And my job is to commend you to the real magic of this particular world. Not to Spiderman and She-ra, the cartoon avatars of fantastical power, but to the genuine romance of this world and of our hearts. My job is to make you and Rebecca students of your possibilities, unconcerned about the plausibility of finding rabbits in hats.)

''Why, of course there's such a thing as magic, Joshie,'' I said, reaching back behind his ear to retrieve a quarter.

''Thanks, Daddy,'' he said, running ahead, having explained it all.

HOW TO PRETEND YOU'VE NEVER SEEN YOUR KIDS BEFORE

Nature is remarkably evenhanded. At about age twelve kids start being embarrassed by their parents, but what they don't realize is that for a dozen years before that, parents spend much of their time being embarrassed by their children. Some advice for dealing with public spectacles.

WALPURGISNACHT AT WENDY'S

You saunter into the restaurant puffed up with pride about your kids, imagining the world gazing at them with envious pleasure that at least they're part of the same species as children such as these. You sit down in a booth and the waitress scurries up to you, tousling your son's hair. The kids are charged up and polite, madly saying please when asking for a hot dog and chocolate milk. For a time all's right with the world.

But as any parent knows things can go south in a big hurry. It's perfectly possible that six minutes from the moment of greatest paternal pride you'll be giving serious thought to slipping out through the kitchen, convinced that the nice cashier will see to it the kids get safely home.

When in restaurants, remember three child facts:

1. Kids have no patience.

2. Kids have no self-control.

3. Especially when they're hungry.

When hungry, impatient people with no self-control are in a restaurant, it's a good bet that something unattractive will happen to that metal serving thing that holds the salad dressing and pickle relish.

A FEW TROUBLING STATISTICS ACCORDING TO A RECENT CBS NEWS/NEW YORK TIMES POLL

- Every 5.9 minutes an American child spits his/her food at his/her sibling in a public place.

- Four out of six waitresses report that they now feel that W. C. Fields was pretty much right about kids.

- Every day American children throw over sixteen pounds of french fries at perfectly innocent customers while screaming, "Daddy, look at that monster lady."

Pardon my frankness, dear reader, but let's not mince words. It's ugly out there on the frontier; it's no country for the squeamish.

THE CRACKER FALLACY

Some parents, believing they can take the edge off kid hunger while waiting for the tuna melts, ask the waitress if she wouldn't mind bringing some crackers—you know, those saltines or Rye Krisps that come wrapped in cellophane. Big mistake. Those crackers don't satisfy kids at all. They just activate the salivary glands and so remind the kids exactly how hungry they are. Often the third or fourth package is eaten with the cellophane still on and is followed by histrionic gagging and spitting. Further, the hopeless nothingness of those crumbs, splayed out across the table, will remind you of the bleakness of life on earth that inspired Beckett.

RESTAURANT COOL QUIZ

For no apparent reason your son spread-eagles himself on top of the table, grabs hold of the ketchup squeeze bottle and threatens to beat himself to death with it. What should you do?

1. Explain that this is a restaurant and this kind of behavior is disturbing to other patrons.

2. Say, "Oh yeah, not if I beat you to death first."

3. Stand up suddenly and, rather in the manner of Claude Rains, say out loud as though to someone in charge, "Exactly what kind of a bistro is this? How do you expect my wife and me to dine if you're going to allow this young man to behave like some sort of hooligan?"

PETER DAY ©1987

Answer Analysis

1. You must be kidding. This polite responsible answer is hopeless with a child gone rogue.

2. This option—threatening to thrash him—will be tempting but it won't work. At this moment he doesn't understand English.

3. The Claude Rains outrage technique is extreme but effective. Though in his state your son will not know exactly what you're saying, even through his mania he'll come to some subcognitive understanding that you're denying knowing him, actually behaving as though you've never seen him before. That's powerful stuff. Within five minutes he'll be telling the waitress the scrambled eggs look tasty.

Parental embarrassment is most likely when children get tired. Once fatigue hits, kids of all ages, races, religions and ethnic groups just plain give up. Unlike adults, who understand that you can't just quit because you're tired, kids will use to powerful effect the Go-Limp, Dead-Weight, My-Bones-Are-Rubber strategy that has been a standby for nonviolent resisters since Gandhi persuaded the British to pack their things. Kids slump to the ground in whining heaps while saying something like, "D-a-a-a-a-d-d-d-y-y, I'm s-o-o-o-o-o tired. C-a-a-a-a-r-r-r-r-r-y-y-y-y-y m-e-e-e-e-e, Daddy." Indeed, some scientists, including Andrew Freddington at MIT, believe that children's unexplained ability to triple their body weight through willful laziness holds the secret of the universe's missing mass.

THE DEAD-WEIGHT RULES

Remember that the kid swoon is a terrorist act, perpetrated to embarrass you outside the church or in the hall of North American mammals.

You'll be tempted, but *under no circumstances drag them by an arm or a leg*. This is just what they want you to do. It makes a great piece of guerrilla theater: some adult goon dragging a kid whose head is bouncing along the concrete. Easy to look like something less than Papa Walton.

The answer is to just keep walking. Remember, Americans don't negotiate with terrorists. When the lump of laundry that used to be your child sees you shrinking into the distance, he'll decide the seventy-five yards to the car is a better bet than a future with the guy who runs the Ferris wheel.

Remember, however, that carrying a weary child can be one of the pleasures. It makes you feel strong.

OF THE ZOOM LENS AND PHOTO OPS

Most often the obligation to take pictures falls to Daddy. These days, with all the camera technology available, an ambitious daddy who's got a few thou to blow can. He can become a familial Spielberg, recording everything from baby's first steps right up through baby's first husband.

But lots of fathers get really stupid with cameras, behaving as though, unless there's a photographic record of young Dylan riding that goat, he may actually never have been to the kiddie zoo at all.

DADDY COOL CAMERA COMMANDMENTS

I. Thou Shalt Never Suggest That Anyone Say "Cheese."

II. Thou Shalt Never Suggest That Anyone Ever Say Any Variant of "Cheese."

There are fathers who ask kids to say, "I love bumble-
bees," or "Uncle Phil has bony knees." I once even
heard a father—a V.P. from Bear Stearns—suggest
"Money, money—if you please." Remember: *When
children smile deliberately they cease to look like your
children and start to look like extras from* Friday, the
13th.

III. **Thou Shalt Never Take a Picture of**
(a) a child wearing his daddy's shoes, or
(b) a child in the bathtub.
I know their naked wet exuberance will appeal to you
but on film these shots always look pathetic. There
are never as many bubbles as you think.

IV. **Thou Shalt Never Interrupt Anything to Take a
Picture.**
The point is to catch your children at play in the fields
of the Lord, not to ask them to imitate the joyful insouci-
ance they were until moments before when you inter-
rupted them. Words to live by: *Lead your life first,
record it when you can.*

There's a good reason we can never quite capture on
film those moments which seem such perfect photo ops. It
has nothing to do with the fact that the camera is always in
the car. It's because the moment we're after doesn't exist.
It is mere fancy, a paternal imagining, made of their
mother's voice, the color of light in the late fall backyard,
the smell of Oreos, the taste of baby sweat. That moment
is an urgent illusion, the alchemy of a passionate mind.
"Only the heart can see clearly," quoth the Little Prince.
"What is essential is invisible to the eye."

OF DADDY AND DOUGH

Before fatherhood there are many retail operations you just don't notice. Before fatherhood your needs are male and predictable—blue jeans, dozen eggs, work boots, six-pack—a minimalist equipping of merely yourself. Ah, but after you're a father, the American world of consuming opens up before you like a land of dreams—polo shirts, thermometers, little pink shoes, strained carrots, Mallomars, socket covers, stupid toys of every description, marvelous toys of same, strollers, Snugglies and Spiderman pajamas, beach balls, baby oil and teensy-weensy toothbrushes—a dazzling catalog of unfamiliar abundance. In short, becoming a father makes you a customer for just about anything. The mere fact that you now have a child transforms the guy selling waddling penguins outside the train station into a business associate.

Needless to say, lots of guys have trouble dealing with the financial left hook of a child: The $2,250 tax deduction just doesn't help much. For those guys the only cool thing is a second job. But even guys who have plenty of bread

often have psychological stress dealing with the juvenile financial hemorrhage. It's important to remember the Daddy Cool Money Mantra: *The kids are what the money's for. After this comes old age and death.*

Every time you spend $209 on overalls and shoes that will fit until Wednesday, say to yourself, "The kids are what the money's for. After this comes old age and death." It'll cheer you up.

SEIZING THE HIGH GROUND

Lots of fathers spend too much time fending off requests, having to respond, usually negatively, to questions such as, "Daddy, can we buy the Avenging Angel Glowing Death Sword? It's only $19.95." Our mistake is in allowing ourselves to be put in a passive negative position. We've got to seize the initiative. Don't wait for your daughter to request a $49.95 electronic speaking dinosaur. Rather, for no good reason bring home a Mickey Mouse coloring pad and some Mickey Mouse coloring pencils. This accomplishes two things:

1. You get to seem like a generous guy for $3.95 instead of $49.95 and, more important:

2. You let your daughter know that she's not the only one who's trying to come up with ideas for things on which to spend money. If she senses you're also looking for opportunities to waste dough, she may kick back a bit, feel less anxious about the possibility that something worth owning will escape her attention and so devote a few of her waking thoughts to something other than coveting her neighbor's toys.

THE CROCKETT CHARGE

Legend has it that when facing hundreds of Indians Davy Crockett and his friend Georgie Russell would use a tactic that came to be called the Crockett Charge. The two of them would bellow commands to imaginary regiments, thereby convincing the Indians that they were facing thousands of the king's finest, causing them to break and run. The Crockett Charge is about the false impression of strength. The Daddy Cool money trick is to concentrate limited financial assets to create an impression of strength.

Plan a special outing—to the zoo, the amusement park, the circus. Plan it six, ten, twelve weeks ahead of time. Put aside $5, $10, $15 a week to be spent at that outing. And then, when the day of the outing comes, spend all of it, every penny of it, spend it with compulsive brio. Here too, don't wait for them to ask. Suggest to Brenda that she might want a kangaroo paperweight or to little Timmy that a gorilla wastebasket would look neat in his room. For that one day make no decision based on cost. Remember the mantra: *After this comes old age and death*. You'll feel better.

The trick is to be *wealthy,* which has nothing to do with money. Just take pleasure in modest things. My father used to make drinking a glass of milk feel like a birthday party. I don't know how he did it; he's the only grown-up I've ever heard use the word "scrumptious." This isn't to say that you ought to act like you've got dough if you don't. After all, no child can possibly grow up healthy unless he hears, "No, sorry, babe," at least once a year.

But you've got to be sure that's not the only sound your girl hears. In short, get the kid launched, out of your house, without an attitude about money. She should feel neither entitled to it nor deprived of it. Let the world teach her such vulgar lessons. Nobody has ever learned anything life-enhancing about money from her father. Daddy's not about money; he's about something else.

Consider:

"Hold On, I've Got a Nickel...Yup, Yup, and Two Cents Ri-i-i-ght Here": Being an Essay on the Perils of Using Exact Change

There are two types of people in the world: people who poke through their pockets or purses, looking for the twenty-nine cents of $5.29, and those who don't, who hand the guy a ten-spot and can live with seventy-one cents in coins. The first group is mostly female; the second is mostly men who jingle all the time. *Exact change is not cool.* It saves you no money and changes the first line of your daughter's memoirs dramatically.

First line of child's memoirs if Daddy doesn't use exact change: "I remember each time my father sat down with me there was a great clatter of coins. Cuddling with Daddy was like hitting the jackpot."

First line of child's memoirs if Daddy uses exact change: "When I think of my father I recall him poking, probing, grubbing ferretlike through his pockets for a nickel he rarely found."

No, Daddy's not about money.

PIGGYBACK COOL

ON THE NECESSITY OF BEING SUPERMAN

The subject of piggyback strikes right to the heart of Daddy Cool. It addresses the fundamental question "Is it all right for Daddy to be tired?" The fundamental answer is no. Uncle Fred can be tired. Daddy can't.

Oh, I know we have all, men and women, been made cripples by the myth of the tireless male. We are locked in some fantasy world of the super he-man. So be it. For my money I would rather my daughter's eulogy for me include the phrase "One piggyback, coming right up," than "Not now, Rebecca, Daddy's tired."

FATIGUE QUIZ

Which of the following guys ever ran out of gas?

1. Rocky Balboa in *Rocky I*

2. Rocky Balboa in *Rocky II*

3. Rocky Balboa in *Rocky III*

4. Rocky Balboa in *Rocky IV*

5. None of the above

Now, of course, we are made of flesh and bone. No real human is capable of giving piggyback rides on demand, especially when your girl hits forty pounds as you hit forty years. So you've got to use indirection, sleight of hand. Make them think you're a piggyback kind of guy. It's all right to be tired, just not in front of the children. Our best hope, facing the piggyback urge of a three-year-old, is to change the subject with vigor.

Child: "Daddy, Daddy, Daddy, give me a piggyback."
Acceptable answers other than, "Sure thing, hop aboard":

1. "Piggyback? That reminds me of the time I danced on the back of a pig." (Stories aren't easy but they don't demand movement and can be told with a glass of Dewar's by your side.)

2. "Piggyback? Not now...let's save that for the Piggyback Festival on Saturday. Let's make a Play-Doh snowman." (They'll forget the festival.)

In brief, the trick is to be so enthusiastic about something else that they'll feel as though they've had a piggyback ride. Incidentally, anytime you actually have the energy to give piggyback rides, don't wait for them to ask. Offer. It'll pay off down the road.

TALKING **C**OOL

OF "YUMMY" AND "YUP"

There are two important facts about cool talk:
1. It's tough, lean, mean, the hip slang-poetry of the streets, station house, barracks, and boardroom.
2. There ain't much of it.

Fact is, cool guys don't say much. They can go for weeks without saying anything more than "A man's gotta do what a man's gotta do." The strong silent type is the American natural, arguably the most powerful male icon of them all. Of course, once you become a father, cool talk can easily become a memory. Not only do you start sounding more like Shari Lewis than Rhett Butler but you turn from a man of few words into a chatterbox of many, including "yucky" and "chubba-wubba." Consider just a few examples of the sugaring of what once was a manly vocabulary.

Before you were a father a rare steak was "goddamn good"; after you're a father it's "yummy." Before you were a father a bullet in the leg was "just a scratch"; after you're a father it's a "Band-Aid boo-boo." Before paternity your penis was nobody's business; after, it's a "willy-worm." Before kids you are "I"; after them you are "Daddy."

But daddies need not despair. There is a way around the Captain Kangarooing of your verbal style. There are corrective measures that can be taken.

THE TALKING COOL
RESCUE PROGRAM

1. Ask Mommy, I mean your wife, to secretly make a tape recording of your conversations. This won't be a happy experience; you'll hear yourself using words like "oops." But it's necessary. Like the alcoholic, the vocabulary wimp has to know he's sick.

2. Make a deliberate attempt to sneak cool phrases into conversations with your kids. For example, at your daughter's sixth birthday, after everybody else drones through "Happy Birthday to You," catch her eye, raise your Kermit cup and say, "Here's mud in your eye, good-lookin'." She will, of course, have no idea what you're talking about but that's okay. You're the one who's trying not to sound like Sesame Street's Grover.

TALKING COOL QUIZ

SCENE: You come around the corner and find your son poised, Crayola in hand, about to draw a picture of his imaginary friend, Fred, on the wall. You should:

1. Tell him not to write on the wall.

2. Go silently over to him, wrest the crayon firmly but gently from his hand and go about your business.

3. Ask him what his plans are.

4. Challenge him to write on the wall with "Go ahead, make my day."

The correct answer is 4. Though there is something cool about simply taking the crayon, quoting Eastwood is preferable. Granted, your son won't know exactly what you're talking about, but, believe me, he'll get the message. Just using the phrase will get you back in touch with your cool, begin the process of decutesifying your diction.

OTHER COOL PHRASES TO DROP IN CONVERSATION

1. Come and get me, copper.

2. You're takin' the fall, sweetheart.

3. Frankly, Scarlett, I don't give a damn.

4. Semper fi.

Some will argue that our uncool diction is far less appalling than the fact that today's fathers—driven by memories of remote monosyllabic fathers—are always talking. I recently heard a father of two sons burst through the door offering to explain—for no apparent reason—exactly how the Mazda rotary engine differs from the traditional piston engine. The younger boy slipped down behind an ottoman and crawled to freedom in the kitchen. These days lots of fathers, determined to be nurturing, bother their children mercilessly, swamping them in paternal attention and enthusiasm that is often a poor substitute for simple silence.

HOW-TO-DO-THE-ZOO-LIKE-SPENCER-TRACY QUIZ

Your daughter has bolted ahead, having caught sight of the gorilla. You catch up with her and say:

1. "Isn't that gorilla marvelous, Judy? It's just like the one in the book at home."

2. Nothing.

The correct answer is 2. A gorilla requires no explanation. If she should for some reason ask you what you make of the gorilla, say something with an understated Spencer Tracy let's-not-get-carried-away simplicity like "That's a fine animal, doll." But better to say nothing. Silence is golden. Not the silence of too little affection, but a respectful silence, the silence on the rim of the Grand Canyon. Don't insist that the world be magic; just let it be.

OFFICE **C**OOL

OF T. BOONE PICKENS AND BUNDLES OF JOY

The surge of daddy enzymes can undo even the most promising career.

Consider the stereotypical corporate big shot—a no-nonsense, sorry-but-we-have-to-let-you-go guy. Not exactly a portrait of cootchy-cootchy-coo. It's a long way from the corporate shark to the guy shaking a seersucker monkey over a playpen. But becoming a daddy need not be fatal to your career. Indeed, it can even on occasion be turned to corporate advantage. But first a few Corporate Cool Don'ts.

THE THREE COMMANDMENTS OF CORPORATE COOL

I. Thou Shalt Not Mention Anything Anatomical About Birth.
Not Lamaze classes, not Braxton-Hicks contractions, certainly not anything to do with labor.

Rarely does a boss respond to the sound of the word "cervix" with, "How does a vice-presidency sound, Hal?" Surely no man who mentions any part of his wife's body in public can be trusted with the Southeast territory. Besides, most modern guys only say the word "breast-feeding" to prove how liberated they are. Remember: *Cool guys don't have to prove anything to anybody.*

II. Thou Shalt Never Show a Picture of a Newborn Baby.

Better yet, never take a picture of a newborn baby. There is no such thing as a three-minute-old beauty. Let's face it—a flat head makes *pretty* a bit of a reach. When looking at a picture of brand-new Margie, there is nothing anybody can say that is both true and sincere. Please, no pictures in the office.

III. Thou Shalt Never Talk About How Little Sleep You're Getting.

Only wimps need sleep. Which brings us to the greatest of all paternal career threats: fatigue.

ROCK-A-BYE, DADDY

During the first few months (or years) of fatherhood you will feel as though you're part of a sleep-deprivation experiment at Yale. You will fall asleep everywhere—in the shower, while you're eating, while you're being mugged. Your dreams will feature drinking yourself into unconsciousness. This is not good for the career. Young lions are bright and alert. Their eyes are on the main chance, not the couch in the boss's office. So a few survival strategies:

1. The Closed Door Charade

If you feel sleep coming on in your office, wait for the phone to ring and answer it with a vigorous hello, while cutting off the caller. Then say, "Hold on, just a sec," ask your assistant to close your office door, lie down on the floor and take an eight-minute nap. Because you haven't closed the door sheepishly, others will assume one of four things:

1. You're having a chat with a woman you probably won't mention to your wife.

2. You're talking to a doctor about test results.

3. You're hammering out the details of a golden parachute.

4. You're advising DOD on state-of-the-art weaponry.

Though there are employers who flat don't approve of closed doors, most will have concern for a guy who's talking to a doctor and grudging admiration for a guy who is doing any of the other three. Think about it: Isn't any of these guesses about you less damaging than the no-doubt-about-it sight of your head between your stapler and your in-box?

2. Yell for Success: The Uses of Volume
Once you're a father, yawning will become a part of your daily office routine. When you feel one coming on, raise your voice for no good reason. It doesn't matter what you shout, though the following three sentences are particularly effective:

1. "By golly, that's a handsome suit, Kalmbach."

2. "And you call yourself a traffic manager?"

   And when in Georgia:
3. "How 'bout them Dawgs?"

The point is that God has arranged it so that we can't raise our voices and yawn at the same time. It doesn't matter that yelling is not your style. These are desperate times. Indeed, the yelling which you've adopted as a defense may actually enhance your career. The fact is, the reason you're not the boss already is that you spend too little time yelling.

CORPORATE GROOMING

It is inevitable that you will one day arrive at work with some sign of your kids on your suit or perhaps in your hair. The trick here, as in so many situations, is to seize the high ground. When you see your boss notice a spot on your Countess Mara tie, rather than explain with something like "Oops, the occupational hazards of being a daddy," just plain solve the problem. Don't explain; Bogey never did. Take off your tie and toss it in the wastebasket. This move demonstrates just the kind of let's-get-this-done style you can bring to the Mercedes account. Remember: *All bosses respect people who throw out clothes.*

A WORD ABOUT POCKETS

Unreported among the changes that come with fatherhood is the fact that your pockets cease being yours. Before paternity there is something sincere between a man and his pockets. But when a man has children his pockets become their property, not his. He can put on the blue pinstripe, reach into the pocket and, without even looking, re-create that after-work picnic in the park. His pockets are sticky museums, a fact not without its professional perils.

A CAUTIONARY QUIZ

You are about to shake on the biggest deal of the year. You take your hand out of your pocket and discover Mr. Potatohead's eyeglasses hanging from your pinky as you are about to pump hands. You:

1. Pretend not to notice.

2. Tell him they are a little corporate memento, something your PR people cooked up.

3. Say, "I'm sorry but those aren't part of the deal. Those belong to Mr. Potatohead."

The right answer is 3. Any other response suggests you can't be trusted.

KITCHEN **C**OOL

OF PANCAKES AND THE QUANTUM CARROT

Fact: The kitchen isn't cool.

I know, all the great chefs are men. But what everybody who's trying to get you into the kitchen forgets to mention about the great chefs of the world is (a) they're French and (b) they don't have a great record when it comes to rescuing MIAs. Bogart had it written in his contract that he never had to appear in the kitchen. Hell, John Wayne never even appeared indoors. No, kitchens aren't cool. They're just so much space that isn't the garage.

Nevertheless, once you become a father, you'll find yourself spending more time in the kitchen. Indeed, once you're a father, your whole relationship with food changes. One minute before your child is born you just plain liked eating it; one minute afterward, it seems as though you spend every waking hour chopping food into quark-sized, chokeproof pieces, up to your eyebrows in cereal, mixing sweet potatoes, zucchini and applesauce in pureed combination that would make a surgeon daddy queasy.

The biggest problem men face when cooking for kids is the Food Group Problem. Although before becoming a father any vaguely alert man can tell you that cheese and yogurt are in the same food group, somehow once fatherhood arrives, most men lose that simple ability. I once gave my son a hearty zucchini, broccoli and string-bean mash. When he remarked that dinner looked "all green like Kermit" I imagined the wellness of those vegetables coursing through his body. He allowed how he preferred dinner the way Mommy made it.

DADDY COOL KITCHEN QUIZ

1. Which of the following foods has protein?
   a. Chicken McNuggets
   b. Chicken Sticks

   c. Cheerios

   d. Applesauce

   e. "Where I come from, we don't like guys who ask a lot of questions."

2. Which of the following foods is rich in vitamin A?
   a. Chicken McNuggets
   b. Chicken Sticks
   c. Cheerios
   d. Carrots
   e. Vitamin what?

3. Which is the best drink for a child with an upset stomach?
   a. Orange juice
   b. Apple juice
   c. Ginger ale
   d. Skim milk
   e. Bourbon—no ice, no glass

4. When may a three-year-old have a cookie?
   a. After lunch for dessert
   b. After dinner if he eats his yams
   c. What is this, Russia?

In each case, the last answer is the cool answer. Cool guys don't overthink in the kitchen. It's bad enough to be there at all.

THE SATURDAY MORNING PANCAKE CLUB

It's 6:20 A.M., Saturday. Daddy time. Mommy sleeps late (8:15, if she's lucky). Daddy is up, flailing around in his robe, crawling desperately through a box of toys in search of diversion, arriving courtesy of some tribal urge in front of a big ceramic bowl. "How 'bout some of Daddy's special pancakes, dolly?" you say.

"Daddy, let's have broccoli pancakes. I love broccoli," she replies, clambering up on a stool step to help you mix the batter. The Daddy Cool response is:

1. "Broccoli and pancakes don't really go together, honey."

2. "No, let's have broccoli when Mommy gets up. Mommy loves broccoli."

3. "Hey, let's give it a try."

The right answer is 3. Lighten up, Daddy. We make the decisions around here, not some stupid folk wisdom that says pancakes don't go with broccoli, that Aunt Jemima combined with vegetables could ignite the earth's atmosphere. But we're not trying to raise a kid who takes another guy's word for it. Make the broccoli pancakes. She'll hate them all by herself.

Designer Pancakes
Lots of fathers have a pancake specialty. My brother's kids rave about his peanut butter pancakes. But even cooler than a special flavor is a special shape. I began as a pancake sculptor quite by accident when the edges of three pancakes merged in a pan and I decided to try to flip them over together, one large Rheingold beer logo. When I dropped them on Josh's plate he squeaked, "Daddy, you made Mickey Mouse." Damned if I hadn't. There was Disney's rodent in flour, milk and eggs. From that day to this I've never looked back.

A Pancake Cool Sampler

FOR YOUR DAUGHTER: Minnie Mouse (smaller ears)

FOR CHRISTMAS: Frosty the Snowman

FOR SAINT PATRICK'S DAY: Shamrock pancakes

FOR THE EIGHTH BIRTHDAY: You get the idea

BERT AND **E**RNIE **C**OOL

A Confessional Guide to Who's Who

Any father who would be cool has to be a quick study; he has to be able to identify thousands of kid media figures who become—suddenly and without permission—part of his life. Before fatherhood, Charlotte was one of the Brontë sisters; now she's E. B. White's writing spider. Before fatherhood, Pat the Bunny was just a legbreaker from the south end.

Believe me, keeping the new cohort of juvenile characters straight is no snap. Why, from the bear species alone Daddy has to recognize Baloo, Winnie the Pooh, the Care Bears, Smokey and Yogi, the Fozzie of Muppet fame, the Berenstains, the Gummi Bears, Teddy Ruxpin and some creature named Kissy Fur. He must know as well the dogs and the cats, some of whom wear hats, the turtles like Yentle, the little lambs and high-hoped rams, the monkeys, the donkeys, the birds who speak words, frogs who go courtin' and an elephant named Horton, a pachyderm named Dumbo, 'nuf wolves to make you numbo. Consider that the Cowardly Lion is also a chicken. It's a taxonomic tumult.

And the animals are just the beginning. Daddies also have to have the superheroes and the baddies down cold. They have to recognize He-man, She-ra and Galtor, this avenging hero of life, that reluctant monster of doom. They even have to know Spiderman's real name (Peter Parker).

But identifying the animals and droids is a can of corn compared with keeping track of Bert and Ernie, the Kramden and Norton of *Sesame Street*. I confess. I was for two years incapable of telling them apart.

I tried everything—mnemonic devices of all sorts—but nothing worked. I was once wrong eleven times in a row, a feat against which the odds are—according to my mathematician friend who has no children—beyond calculation. Finally, after enduring Hitchcockian nightmares of being unable to recognize my own kids, after hypnosis, after our Rebecca at eighteen months started coming up to me, shaking her Ernie doll and saying, "Not Bert, Daddy," after Jody pointed out that I had lost my power to a pair of striped puppets, I stumbled on the obvious and foolproof method for telling who's who.

The liberating revelation: Everybody knows that a guy named Bert is short, stout and affable and a guy named Ernie is tall, thin and fussy. But the people at the Children's Television Workshop have cross-christened their creatures. So the trick is to go contrarian. If you think it's Bert, it's Ernie; if you think it's Ernie, it's Bert.

I swear.

DISCIPLINE COOL

HOW TO GET A DRAW WITH SOMEONE SMALL

Let's face it, discipline is a tough topic for fathers. There's not a man in this country who doesn't fantasize about large crowds of people daily doing our bidding. All men dream about being an authority—a CEO/general/quarterback hybrid of Henry Ford, George Patton and Jim McMahon. Consequently, when we become fathers and our appetite for influence—thwarted daily on the job and almost everywhere else—runs into the contrary reality of a thirty-six-pound person in a polo shirt, it can be an occasion of despair. We imagine the Charge of the Light Brigade, young men surging to their deaths because we said so, and we can't get Melinda out from under the sink.

For a time, after the Aquarian revolution of the late sixties/early seventies, discipline was in decline. But with the eighties headed into the nineties, discipline is back and better than ever. And the atavistic fact is that the most useful lessons of Discipline Cool are alive in the good-old-fashioned martial spirit, the muse of unquestioned because-I'm-your-father authority.

FEERS DAY & 1987

A DISCIPLINARY DISQUISITION:
ON "BECAUSE I SAID SO"

Many fathers spend a lot of time these days explaining themselves to their children. Big mistake. Neither Winston Churchill nor Mary Poppins ever explained anything to anybody.

Hypothetical

Your daughter is perched on top of your desk, riffling through tax returns, subpoenas and unpaid bills.

You say—simply and directly—ever hopeful that's all it will take, "Get down from there, Melinda." She gives some standard kid response like "But, Daddy, I'm looking for something very important. Don't ask me what it is, Daddy, because it's private.''

"Melinda, I said, get down from there,'' you say, only slightly louder than the first time.

"But why, Daddy?'' she says, a daring little girl whose spirit will serve her well someday but is right now a real threat to her well-being. It is at this point that many modern daddies in one move manage to both lose their souls and betray their children by...

... answering the question.

Answering the question is a no-win decision. The fact is that no answer makes any sense to children. First, no child believes she can get hurt. Second, kids don't understand the notion of decorum—the simple idea that desks aren't for climbing. Further, if you let her get you into a discussion of whether or not desks are for climbing, before long you'll come unglued and begin questioning all the marvelous little assumptions—like the one that shoes should be on your feet, not stuffed with grapes—which to the childish anarchic mind appear foolish, but merely make life possible. And finally, kids know nothing from audits, so they won't understand that you need those papers if you're to have any chance of keeping the IRS from seizing your home.

The key to discipline is to retreat behind a time-honored parental cliché, the Mommy and Daddy standby, "Because I said so." When Melinda asks why she has to get off the desk, please don't explain. Just say in a no-nonsense bark, "Because I said so." Yes, that phrase that drove you mad as a child. First, her question is a smart-ass question, and second, all you're really saying is that she's got to get off the desk because life needs rules. Otherwise, we're all bound for chaos, pawns at the entropic mercy of the Second Law of Thermodynamics.

"Because I said so" is merely the most forceful and nostalgic of Daddy disciplinary phrases. Other retro-Dad riffs which can be used to good effect are:

1. "If I have to come up there..."
2. "This discussion is over..."
3. "I'm not asking you, Kiki..."

Make no mistake. No cool daddy is a thug. Once Melinda clambers like a good girl down from the desk, you can—and should—explain about the g-force with which from that height her head might have hit the floor. You might also tell her everything you know about that nincompoop Witherspoon from the IRS. You can even try to explain that unless life has rules it is mere protoplasm.

But explaining yourself before compliance is giving her more power than she really wants. Down deep, no three-year-old wants to think she can talk her parents out of things. If you suggest that your authority needs the validation of logic, you'll have your kid lying in bed wondering who's in charge here, and whether you can handle those crooks from the IRS.

DISCIPLINE COOL QUIZ

Eight-year-old Julian is flinging baby peas at his sister, using a not-stupidly-designed catapultlike contraption featuring a teaspoon launcher pivoted on a bread-stick fulcrum. You tell him to stop. Though he clearly hears you in time to abort the pea he now has loaded, he fires it as though he didn't. He looks at you to see exactly how stupid you are. You:

1. Tell him peas are food, not weapons.

2. Tell him that, though you admire his catapult, Ruthie is not an acceptable target.

3. Clip him in the back of the head, catching just the barest wisp of his cowlick while making a face that will scare him to death.

4. Tell him to leave the table instantly and to prepare a written apology to his sister, who—unless you have missed something—did nothing to deserve a vegetable to the throat.

Answer Analysis

Answer 1 is wrong. He knows peas aren't weapons. This situation requires no explaining. He defied you on purpose. He's seeing how serious you are about this family.

Answer 2 is also wrong. Complimenting the design of his catapult seems to suggest that engineering flair can mitigate rudeness. It can't. Not in this house, pally.

Answer 3 is wrong, too. The threatening nonblow is a time-honored Daddy tradition and, given your status in the family, is not without effectiveness, but, when all is said and done, there is little less cool than menacing somebody you could put in your pocket. General rule: *If you use your physical power over your child, you lose your real power.*

Answer 4 is the Daddy Cool answer. Banishment is a key disciplinary concept. The message: No savages can play on this team. Further, the written apology is a nice gimmick for two reasons: (a) writing down that he's sorry has a finality that can help him put the whole thing behind him and (b) kids will use such ingenuity to write an apology that satisfies Dad while admitting no wrongdoing that it can't help but enhance their eventual scores on the verbal SATs.

PURSUING HAPPINESS:
AN AMERICAN DISCIPLINARY MEDITATION

Remember: Cool is not about rules. Clyde Barrow, Mad Dog Earl, Butch and Sundance, none of them ever made much of a fuss about rules. Quite the opposite. Cool is about freedom.

Our forefathers didn't come here because they were looking to rely on local zoning ordinances. They came here for Wyoming, where 'bout the only discipline a man needed was the guts to follow his dream. As far as fatherly discipline is concerned, the key is to make as few rules as possible. Consider the Bill of Rights. Just ten ideas. Minimal. Straightforward. Potent. Plenty of room for eccentricity of spirit.

SCREAMING, YELLING,
CONFRONTATION COOL

One of the most important things to remember about disciplining your children is that, while it's important to be firm and not take the easy route of giving kids the car keys, it's also important to resist the tough-guy hard-liner who lingers not far below the surface in most men.

My daughter, Rebecca, and I have extravagant disagreements on occasion. Once a week her eighteen-month-old wisdom will instruct her to climb on the top of the table while her mother and father and brother are trying to have dinner. There is nothing—I mean, nothing—that can change her mind. She's an addict in need of a fix. I'm talking desperate—shrieking, yelling, macaroni à la Edvard Munch. Mommy retreats to the linen closet wondering why she got married in the first place.

Remember a negotiating technique that has been used successfully for centuries by business people and diplomats. Change the venue. Just call off the war. Get up suddenly, with her freaking out in your arms, turn on the stereo and dance with her on your shoulder. For a while she'll keep yelling because that's what babies do, but then slowly it'll dawn on her that you've offered her a way out, peace with honor. She didn't lose the battle. Neither did you. It just went away.

In general when your kids are *in extremis* remember one simple fact—these are your children. Don't win. If they get the sense you're not out to bust their chops, they'll lighten up.

Similarly, make a point of changing the rules when they least expect it. So if 8:30 is bedtime, some Friday, after he's tucked in, having accepted the family rule, sidle into his room and ask him if he'd like to listen to the new Disney tape. He'll sit up, look around as though he's being set up, say a tentative "Sure, Daddy," and come to believe that rules are not the enemy but rather a slavish attachment to them.

ON WASHING THE CHILDREN AND THE CAR

Children are time machines. It's well known that they speed time up by growing up in an instant. But they can also slow time down—ask any parent about how the hour before bedtime actually takes three weeks to transpire. Once you have kids, you will have no time. No time to eat your dinner, shine your shoes, comb your hair, think a thought. Only ecclesiastical time to be born and time to die remains. Trust me, you won't have a minute to cast away stones.

Consequently, mere survival demands that you learn to do more than one thing at a time. A few suggestions for things daddies might productively combine in the hope of accomplishing enough to have a life.

BATHING YOUR SON AND WASHING YOUR CAR

It's August, 84° at dusk. Strip the little guy and hose him

down with the Chevy. He'll love it. Besides, a quick once-over with a chamois does great things for his skin.

Reading the Newspaper and Telling Bedtime Stories

Of course, federal indictments of the Gotti clan are not the stuff of bedtime tales. But with a little imagination lots of news and features from the daily newspaper can be turned into something for the kids. Throw in a kid word now and then—change junk bonds to marbles, Kalashnikov rifles to secret message decoders—and Pennzoil vs. Texaco and Mets vs. Cards become real tales.

Further, if your job demands that you know something about what's happening in the world, you owe this combination of activities to your kids. Out of work is never cool.

PAYING YOUR BILLS AND MAKING LOVE TO YOUR WIFE

Nobody likes to interrupt an ascent to heaven. But the very fact that you're making love to your wife at all suggests that you've gotten lucky beyond most Daddy luck. You mustn't tempt fate by insisting on an uninterrupted encounter. If you do, you'll never get a chance to pay your bills and you'll end up with some guy on the phone asking your daughter if "the deadbeat" is at home. So excuse yourself, take a break and make good on a debt or two.

Try to think of the necessity of doing two (or even three) things at once as a challenge to your ingenuity. After all, anybody might have happened upon the theory of relativity if he didn't have to worry about getting Mandy to soccer practice. But can you do it all? Can you transform both physics as we know it *and* the angel costume for the Christmas play? Probably not, but it's a challenge worth a man's energy.

Of course, there is an upside to all the damage kids do to time. Often, riding on a bus with your child, shampooing her hair, answering earnest naive questions about people's shoes, getting a haircut with your son, often while presiding, over a circus of bending and tending, you can actually feel time being lifted from your neck. You'll feel in a particular mundane moment that there is only now.

Kids are the best weapon against time. Be their father. Now.

PAIN COOL

OF OUCH AND ZEN

In general, being a father is not physically painful. But there are several rarely-spoken-of parental agonies. The worst of them is one of the nasty little secrets of fatherhood, the truth that dare not speak its name lest legions of men take a fearful skip on paternity. It has to do with chest hair or, more precisely, with what happens when someone who weighs fifty-three pounds uses your breastplate as a place on which to plant a humid sneaker in order to change direction in midflight.

> SCENE: Your son, your daughter, their cousin Jane and the kid from next door are careering, banging, shouting around the house, apparently reenacting the chariot race from *Ben-Hur*. Suddenly your son comes around the corner at full tilt, pursued by his companions. He heads right toward you, leaps into the air, shouts, "And now back to the Colosseum," stomps a rubber-shod foot onto your sternum, turns 180°, pushes off with a thrust per square inch worthy of the space shuttle and bolts away.

For an instant you feel nothing but annoyance. But then after a beat you remember that your fourth-grade teacher smelled like those purple flowers and you imagine that your heart is going to explode.

It is a moment of such pain that even Amnesty International would rather not talk about it. This experience hurts like the dickens even for the fortunate few daddies who have no hair on their bodies. But for the cuddly fuzzy daddies among us, words fail.

Oh, there are other painful moments of daddyhood—being awakened by an Etch-a-Sketch to the frontal lobe springs to mind—but compared to your enemy, the sneaker, they are a shower and a shave. Further, there is nothing anybody can do to prevent the sneaker attack from happening. Any father who spends more than eight minutes a day with his children will be a victim—not once, not twice, but somehow hundreds of times.

There is no hope for your body. No matter what you do, what started out as your grand manly pelt will—by the time your children are grown—end up looking like the fifty-yard line at Lambeau Field. No, you can't prevent it. You can only practice damage control; you can only be prepared.

SNEAKER SURVIVAL STEPS

1. Collapse to Live

Nature has built us to respond to an assault with a counteroffensive. When somebody's foot lands on your heart, your instincts direct you to surge against it. The problem is that even the merest resistance multiplies the force between shoe and chest by a factor of six trillion. By resisting we become, in effect, co-conspirators. The only way to survive is to train our minds and bodies to give in, to overcome our adrenal fight instinct in favor of the adrenal flight instinct. We must, at the instant of contact, collapse immediately to the floor, thereby decreasing the energy coefficient at the point of friction from the level at the core of a hydrogen bomb to the level at the heart of the Bessemer blast furnace. No bargain, I grant you, but it ain't ground zero.

2. Laugh for the Children

Your first instinct will be to roar, rather in the manner of Lear on the heath, yell at your son that you'll rip his lungs out if you catch him. Don't do it. In general, roaring isn't cool.

But you've got to make some sound. If you don't your internal organs will spontaneously fuse.

So force yourself to laugh. Beginning with a wry giggle, build slowly to a hearty chuckle, ascend through a vulgar guffaw and climax at last in a maniacal cackle which will, I promise, give relief and feel like home.

3. Hide to Thrive

You mustn't let your children see you curled up on the floor licking the rug. Crawl somewhere, anywhere you can be alone. Behind the drapes. Under the bed. Into a cord of wood. Then, use the very same Lamaze breathing techniques that helped your wife bring your children into this world of woe, rub saliva (or motor oil if available) on your chest and repeat over and over to yourself that life is durable. You'll be fine—or dead—come morning.

PETERS DAY OF 87

OTHER PAIN SCENARIOS

1. Mine Eyes Have Seen the Gory

You're having trouble sleeping and so, thinking that a shot
of Jack Daniel's might help, you get out of bed and head
for the booze. Out of the bedroom door, down the hall, left
turn, when suddenly . . . inexplicably . . . awesomely . . .
violently. . . your drowsy stupor is devoured by a bolt of
pain that starts at your foot and surges through your leg on
the way to your trunk. You stagger against the wall, grope
for the wall switch, squint into the sudden light and see
sitting there on the floor—for all the world as harmless,
childish as can be—a

  1. Little yellow Duplo block
  2. Little green Barbie hairbrush

3. Little blue fish from that fishing game the kids got at Caldor
4. Little white doohickey
5. Little orange something

Somehow we never manage to step over these little land mines. And somehow we always step on them with acupunctural accuracy, pressing them between foot and floor in the precise spot that will render us momentarily homicidal toward the child who left it there and anybody who has ever owned stock in Toys 'Я' Us.

But with adaptation there is hope. You need not end up gasping for breath, wiping your tears away with flannel sleeve, you need merely master:

The Pensioner's Shuffle

Learn to walk like an old guy wearing slippers with no backs, like any character from a play by Harold Pinter. Scuff your feet right along the floor, thereby transforming a jack driven into your heel into a jack kicked harmlessly against the baseboard. Of course, this gait is a nocturnal pajama-clad survival strategy only. Warning: *Don't let it poison your vigorous manly midday strut.*

2. The Jawbreaker

You're seated. Between your knees is a child, most often between three and five, slumping to the ground, far from cooperating with your efforts to get her into underwear, overalls, socks, sandals, etc. But you're persisting, deliberately loving this child who, you keep reminding yourself, is the whole point of your life. Suddenly *it* happens.

What had been a lifeless whining mass turns into a Saturn rocket, standing straight up and driving her head into your jaw and so causing you to bite—and in that moment, you believe, swallow—your tongue. Your only hope is to:

1. Lie down on the floor immediately and

2. Bang your head repeatedly against it until you lose consciousness.

I promise you this will be less painful than being awake for the next three minutes.

WHAT TO TELL THE KIDS ABOUT WAR, SPORTS, POLITICS, GOD, BUSINESS, SEX AND LOVE

Most fathers spend a lot of time sounding like Henry Kissinger, as though they know something about the world. It matters not that the kids are less interested in the world according to Dad than they are in McDonald's Happy Meals. Our weaknesses for opinion looms over us. Becoming a father seems to trigger a male declamatory gland and a catalog of capital-lettered riffs on the way the world is.

Just before Josh was born Jody confronted me with her suspicion that I would make a son play baseball even if he was afraid of the ball. Though she was wrong in the baseball detail, she had nailed me in broader terms. Indeed, in the months before Josh's birth I often imagined what I would tell him about my parents, about our country, about money, about his mother, about Reggie's night of three homers, about shining his shoes. I had a boatload of notions, a version of the world, to which I hoped my boy would be susceptible. But at the cantankerous moment of his arrival I could almost feel the smoke of opinion giving way to his clarity, so brand-new.

Since then the kids have been a pilgrim's progress to uncertainty. Suddenly I'm in uncool places and making uncool sounds. Suddenly my habits of body and mind, the flaunt of American manhood, that half-baked amalgam of swagger and strength, is sweetly undone by their need. Each day I can feel them allowing me to put away manly things and merely, humbly, honor them with what juice I have.

Every single hallelujah time I do something, however reluctantly, in their service, every time I cuddle up with them or conjure up some story, every time I tend them, every time I go down some road the momentum of maleness had until then made uninviting, there's a payoff— sometimes gaudy, a one-liner for the ages, more often less so, a question, a sound of fear, and most often just the quiet tonic of their company, revealing at once both the common world and the contours of the unseen one.

Cool isn't sure. Cool thinks the world is a tough game to figure.

Cool is listening except when you should talk. Cool is kneeling before their exuberance. Cool is keeping to ourselves the stupidity we so unwittingly cherish. Cool is pitching underhand until they tell you to get serious.

Here's looking at you, Dad.